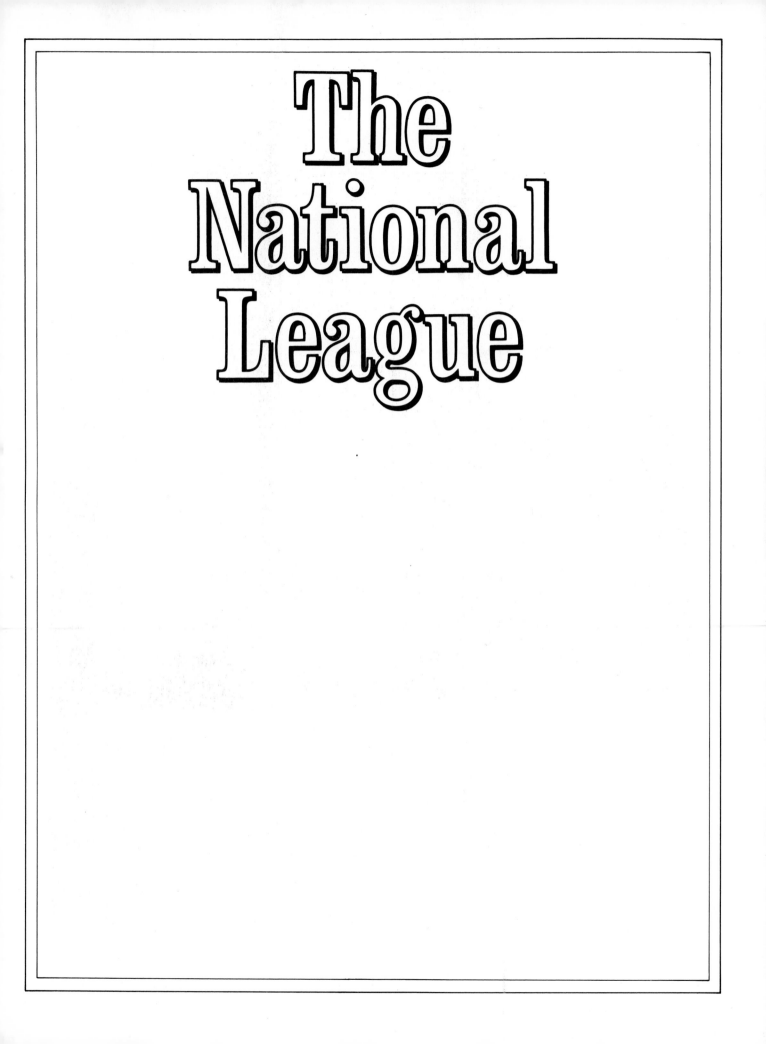

The National League

Willie Mays in 1951.

The National League

An Illustrated History

by Donald Honig

Crown Publishers, Inc.
New York

Published by Crown Publishers, Inc., One Park Avenue, New York, New York 10016,
and simultaneously in Canada by General Publishing Company Limited

Manufactured in the United States of America

Library of Congress Cataloging in Publication Data

Honig, Donald.
The National League, an illustrated history.

1. National League of Professional Baseball Clubs—
History.   I. Title.
GV875.A3H66   1983   796.357′64′0973   83-2072
ISBN 0-517-55041-5

10 9 8 7 6 5 4 3 2 1

First Edition

Design: Robert Aulicino

For my daughter, Catherine

By Donald Honig

Fiction

Sidewalk Caesar
Walk Like a Man
The Americans
Divide the Night
No Song to Sing
Judgment Night
The Love Thief
The Severith Style
Illusions
I Should Have Sold Petunias
The Last Great Season
Marching Home

Nonfiction

Baseball When the Grass Was Real
Baseball Between the Lines
The Man in the Dugout
The October Heroes
The Image of Their Greatness (with Lawrence Ritter)
The 100 Greatest Baseball Players of All Time (with Lawrence Ritter)
The Brooklyn Dodgers: An Illustrated Tribute
The New York Yankees: An Illustrated History
Baseball's 10 Greatest Teams
The Los Angeles Dodgers: The First Quarter Century
The National League: An Illustrated History
The American League: An Illustrated History

For Young Readers

Frontiers of Fortune
Jed McLane and Storm Cloud
Jed McLane and the Stranger
In the Days of the Cowboy
Up from the Minor Leagues
Dynamite
Johnny Lee
The Journal of One Davey Wyatt
An End of Innocence
Way to Go Teddy
Playing for Keeps
Breaking In
The Professional
Coming Back
Fury on Skates
Hurry Home
Running Harder
Going the Distance
Winter Always Comes

Editor

Blue and Gray: Great Writings of the Civil War
The Short Stories of Stephen Crane

Contents

Acknowledgments

I am deeply indebted to a number of people for their generous assistance in photo research and help in gathering the photographs reproduced in this book. Special thanks are due Jack Redding, librarian of the National Baseball Hall of Fame and Museum in Cooperstown, New York, for his interest and his help. Also, to Michael P. Aronstein, president of Card Memorabilia Associates, Ltd., in Amawalk, New York, for the generosity of his assistance and the unique wisdom and enthusiasm he brings to his work. I would also like to thank those big-league ballplayers who allowed the use of pictures from their personal albums. The remaining pictures are from the following sources:

J. J. Donnelly, Pearl River, New York: pp. 290, 299 (left), 314 (right), 316 (left), 318 (left), 319 (top and bottom), 320 (top left and right), 323 (right), 324 (left), 327 (right), 330 (top right), 331 (right), 332 (left), 333 (right), 336 (top left).

Nancy Hogue, Warren, Ohio: pp. 302, 321, 322 (left, top right, bottom right), 323 (top left), 325, 326 (top right), 329 (left), 330 (left, bottom right), 333 (left), 334 (bottom left), 335 (right, bottom left).

Ronald C. Modra, Port Washington, Wisconsin: pp. 328 (top), 331 (bottom left), 335 (top left).

For their good advice and wise counsel, I am indebted to these keen students of baseball history: David Markson, Lawrence Ritter, Stanley Honig, Colin Grotheer, Allan J. Grotheer, and Mary E. Gallagher.

The National League

William A. Hulbert.

1

Beginning

The nation was celebrating its one-hundreth anniversary when the National League went into business in 1876. Professional baseball, as it then existed, was vested in a structure called the National Association of Professional Base Ball Players. Organized in 1871, this enterprise had been getting increasingly less edifying with each passing year. Gambling was heavy, and as a consequence players were accepting bribes to throw games. Drunkenness on the field was not uncommon and there was a lot of rowdyism. Fan interest was high, but there was diminishing faith in the integrity of the game, as well as growing disapproval with its general character.

It was at this point that a Chicago businessman and baseball fan named William Ambrose Hulbert stepped into the picture. Hulbert felt that baseball had a great future in America, but only if the game's reputation was put beyond reproach. Along with Al Spalding, a star pitcher with Boston of the National Association (and later the founder of the sporting goods concern that bears his name), Hulbert conceived and put together the National League of Base Ball Clubs.

Hulbert's first move was to establish four franchises to make up the western sector of his league: Chicago, St. Louis, Cincinnati, and Louisville. Obtaining power of attorney from these clubs, he then traveled east and lined up four more clubs to give the league geographical balance: New York, Boston, Philadelphia, and Hartford. Each one of these cities passed one of Hulbert's basic requirements—that it have a population of no less than 75,000.

If the National League has a proper birth date, it is February 2, 1876, for it was on this date that Hulbert met with representatives of the four eastern teams in the Grand Central Hotel on Broadway in New York City and heard them agree to become part of his proposed eight-team league.

A 70-game schedule was planned, with each team playing the other ten times. The team with the most victories would be declared champion. Emblematic of the championship would be a pennant costing not less than $100.

Over the next 25 years there was a good deal of realignment in the league. Franchises shuffled in and out with dismaying regularity. In the league at one time or another were Providence, Milwaukee, Indianapolis, Buffalo, Cleveland, Syracuse, Troy, Detroit, Worcester, Kansas City, Washington, Pittsburgh, Brooklyn, and Baltimore. By 1899 it was a 12-club lineup. A year later, however, the National League celebrated the turn of the century by finally stabilizing into the 8-club structure that remained undisturbed for the next 53 years: New York, Brooklyn, Boston, and Philadelphia in the East; St. Louis, Cincinnati, Chicago, and Pittsburgh in the West.

No sooner did the league assume its permanent shape, however, than it found itself confronted by a competing operation, the American League. The new league anointed itself with major-league status and immediately plunged into sharp competition with its old, established rival. It was not the first challenge that had been made to the National League's supremacy. From 1883 to 1891 there was the American Association, in 1884 the Union Association, in 1890 the Players' League. Teams came and went, with the players being lured here and there by the most promising checkbooks. The National League outlasted them all, until the arrival of the new league in 1901. There was a lot of squabbling, bitterness, and litigation between the two leagues, with each raiding the rosters of the other.

In 1903 peace was declared and the two rivals even agreed to engage each other in a postseason meeting of their champions called the World Series.

Into the Modern Age

In terms of quality ballplayers, the baseball war was expensive for the National League. Included among the stars who jumped to the American League and never went back were Wee Willie Keeler, Sam Crawford, Elmer Flick, Jimmy Collins, Ed Delahanty, Nap Lajoie, and Jesse Burkett.

Burkett was the batting champion in the National League's first modern season, 1901. The 5'8" left-handed stroker batted .376 for the St. Louis Cardinals (a year later Jesse changed leagues but not cities, signing with the St. Louis American League club). Led by Burkett and shortstop Bobby Wallace, the Cardinals, who finished fourth, topped the league in attendance with nearly 380,000 paid admissions. Wallace, known in his day as "Mr. Shortstop," also jumped to the rival St. Louis club after the 1901 season. In 1906, while playing for the St. Louis Browns, Bobby became baseball's highest-salaried player with paydays amounting to $6,000 per annum, veritable megabucks in those unhurried early-century days.

While the Cardinals may have drawn the most customers and had baseball's premier shortstop, the pennant winners in 1901 were the Pittsburgh Pirates. Pittsburgh rolled in 7½ games ahead of second-place Philadelphia to take the league's first "modern" pennant. The club's top hitter was a twenty-seven-year-old five-year veteran named John Peter ("Honus") Wagner.

One of the reasons Bobby Wallace was still "Mr. Shortstop" was because Honus Wagner had not as yet made that position preeminently his own. In 1901 Wagner played 61 games at short, 24 at third, and 54 in the outfield. Among the many qualities possessed by this ballplaying genius was versatility.

Honus Wagner.

A year later Wagner began playing shortstop on a regular basis and once he did, the standard for the position was established for all time. The muscular, bowlegged, sure-handed powerhouse remains the olympian of the infield.

Wagner, a native of Carnegie, Pennsylvania, was a sweet-natured, modest, folksy character. In his prime he attained a salary of $10,000 and was satisfied. Year after year, when asked by his employers how much he wanted, he said, "Same as last year." He entered the National League with the Louisville club in 1897, batted .344, and was off and running to a peerless career. When Louisville left the league after the 1899 season, Wagner and some of his teammates, most notably player-manager Fred Clarke, third baseman Tommy Leach, and pitcher Deacon Phillippe, joined the Pittsburgh club, giving the Pirates the strongest outfit in the league.

The Pirates won the pennant again in 1902 and 1903. The 1902 Pirates were awesome, winning 103 games and losing just 36 for a .741 winning percentage (the league played a 140-game schedule until 1904), finishing an astonishing 27½ games ahead of second-place Brooklyn. Pittsburgh had the league's leading hitter in Ginger Beaumont (.357), while Wagner led in stolen bases, runs batted in, runs scored, doubles, and slugging average. They also had the home run champion in Tommy Leach, who bashed a modest six homers to lead the league. The pitching staff was topped by 28-game winner Jack Chesbro, while Phillippe and Jesse Tannehill each won 20. With a 16-man player limit in force at the time, pitchers were expected to go the distance. Accordingly, most pitching staffs averaged around 120 complete games a season.

One reason for Pittsburgh's supremacy in 1902 was that they were able to hold on to their star players while other National League clubs were seeing their rosters being raided by the upstart American League. The Phillies, for instance, in second place in 1901, dropped to seventh in 1902 after losing their two best hitters, Elmer Flick and Ed Delahanty, and 20-game winners Al Orth and Red Donahue to the new league.

The Pirates weren't quite as lucky in 1903, losing Chesbro to the newly franchised New York American League entry (then known as the Highlanders, later rechristened Yankees). The Pirates won again, though, behind Wagner's .355 league-leading average and a combined 49 victories from Deacon Phillippe and Sam Leever. But this time the Pittsburgh victory was no cakewalk. There was a new powerhouse building in the league, the New York Giants, a team so brilliantly and possessively managed that they soon became known as John McGraw's Giants.

McGraw, a 5'7" little Napoleon (one of his nicknames; another was "Muggsy," which he hated), had been a star third baseman with the Baltimore Orioles in the 1890s. McGraw joined the Giants in 1902 at the age of twenty-nine, his playing career coming to an end. Midway through the season he took over as manager, a position he held until June 1932. In his 31 years at the helm, he won 10 pennants and had 11 second-place finishes. Only twice was he out of the first division. The record is remarkable; but so was John J. McGraw.

He was brilliant, tyrannical, innovative, and relentless. He made the Giants the most artistically and financially successful team in baseball, the dominant club until the advent of Babe Ruth and the rise of the Yankees in the 1920s. Many of his players hated him; others worshiped him; none ever questioned his baseball acumen. Some, like Casey Stengel and Burleigh Grimes, hard-bitten veterans, did not consider their careers complete until they had played for McGraw, with the all-knowing and fabulously successful Stengel saying in later years that he regarded McGraw as his mentor.

When McGraw took over the Giants in 1902 his top pitcher was a twenty-three-year-old right-hander named Christy Mathewson. The Giants had obtained Mathewson from Cincinnati in a trade two years before for pitcher Amos Rusie, a titan of the 1890s but now at the end of the road. Amos won no games for Cincinnati; Matty won 373 for the Giants.

Tall, handsome, intelligent, manly, Christy Mathewson became the nation's first genuinely admired sports idol. Educated at Bucknell, where he was class president as well as a member of the glee club and literary society, Matty was almost too good to be true, both on and off the diamond. His image was so pure that his wife had to go out of her way to emphasize he was not a "goody-goody." Christy could use profanity with the best of them, took a drink now and then, and was a fierce competitor on the mound. He was one of those rare athletes who was looked up to by his peers for his personal qualities as well as his athletic abilities.

Mathewson possessed all the equipment of a great pitcher. He was fast, threw an almost unhittable curve that broke from the shoulders to the knees with a wicked snap, and virtually pioneered the screwball, which was called a "fadeaway" in those days. Over each of these pitches he had uncanny control. From 1903 through 1914 he won 22 or more games, topping the 30 mark three times, with a peak of 37 in 1908.

Given the dissimilarities in their personalities and backgrounds, McGraw and Mathewson should not have got along. But they did, famously. To the childless McGraw, Matty was like a son. The affection and mutual respect that existed between these two titans of New York baseball was genuine, and when Mathewson died of tuberculosis in 1925 at the age of 45, McGraw was heartbroken.

Behind Matty's 33 wins in 1904 and "Iron Man" Joe McGinnity's 35, McGraw's Giants won the pennant by a comfortable 13-game margin over the Chicago Cubs. John J. won 106 games, setting a new major-league rec-

ord. McGraw also gave his opponents a good dose of his style of play, turning his jackrabbits loose for a total of 283 stolen bases.

A year later the Giants won 105 games, finishing nine up on Pittsburgh. It was one of Mathewson's purest years, the big righty winning 31 and losing just 8, with a 1.27 earned-run average. But what seemed like a looming Giant dynasty was about to be knocked aside by a Chicago Cubs team set to turn loose upon the National League some of the most remarkable pitching baseball has ever seen.

McGraw's pride of 106 wins in 1904 was not only surpassed by the Cubs, but wiped out by a comfortable margin as the Chicagoans won a stunning 116 games, still the major-league record. This was the team of Tinker to Evers to Chance, inscribed in baseball legend by a bit of third-rate poetry celebrating their double-play-making prowess. The infield was far superior to the poetry, though history has recorded many better DP combinations. Nevertheless, they were a smooth-working, highly efficient trio.

Second baseman Johnny Evers was the hustling, chatterbox dynamo of the club. So fiery and garrulous was he on the diamond that shortstop Tinker finally got to the point where he would speak to his teammate only in the line of duty, refusing to speak to Johnny off the field. First baseman-manager Frank Chance set a fine example for his squad in 1906, batting .319 and showing the way to hustle with a league-leading 57 stolen bases. The infield's forgotten man, third baseman Harry Steinfeldt, who gave up a career as a touring minstrel in the 1890s to go into baseball, actually had more pop than any of them, with a .327 batting average and league-high totals in hits and runs batted in.

But it was the pitching staff that commanded. Chance's aces were led by Mordecai ("Three Finger") Brown. Brown, Mathewson's chief rival for league pitching honors in the first decade of the century, had as a child caught his right hand in a threshing machine and emerged with a mangled finger and an ability to make a baseball do wonderfully sharp-breaking things. With this slight improvement upon what nature had already given him, Brown went on to become one of the greatest of pitchers. In 1906 he was 26–6, backed up by lefty Jack Pfeister's 20–8, Ed Reulbach's 19–4, and Carl Lundgren's 17–6. Chance's pitchers logged a collective 1.76 earned-run average, headlined by Brown's almost invisible 1.04. Lundgren, with a 2.21 ERA, was high on the staff.

In an era of tight pitching, the Cub staff was exceptional. The Chicago team batting average of .262 was tops, with five teams batting under .241. All of which made Honus Wagner's .339 league-leading average all the more impressive. It was Wagner's fourth batting championship; he would take four more, the last in 1911 at the age of thirty-seven.

In 1907 the Cubs "slipped" to 107 victories and a 17-game margin over second-place Pittsburgh, where Honus Wagner was ripening with age, taking another batting crown, with a .350 average. Chicago's superb infield helped their pitchers to a 1.73 earned-run average, lowest in National League history. None of Frank Chance's starters—Brown, Orval Overall, Lundgren, Reulbach, Pfeister—posted an ERA over 1.69. It was still very much a pitcher's game in 1907, with Pittsburgh leading the league with a .254 team batting average. The league as a whole batted just .243.

The Cubs took a third straight flag in 1908, but only after one of baseball's most controversial moments. Unlike the previous two years, the Cubs had to battle a tenacious Giant team all summer long. On September 23, with mere percentage points separating the clubs, the Cubs engaged the Giants at the Polo Grounds. With the score 1–1 in the bottom of the ninth, the Giants got a rally going. With two out, they had men on first and third. The runner on first was nineteen-year-old Fred Merkle, given the assignment to play first base that day because the regular, Fred Tenney, had been unable to play.

McGraw's shortstop, Al Bridwell, came to the plate and promptly busted a single to center to score the winning run. But was it the winning run? The Polo Grounds partisans were going wild; but strange things were happening on the field. In order for the run to count, Merkle had to touch second. It was common practice in those situations, however, for the runner on first to head for the clubhouse the moment the winning run scored. As soon as he saw Bridwell's hit land safely, young Merkle sprinted for the clubhouse, located in center field in the Polo Grounds. Johnny Evers, the Cubs' alert second baseman, saw this, called for the ball (according to some people, he got *a* ball, not *the* ball, which was probably rolling around the outfield somewhere), and touched second, thereby turning the base hit into a force play and voiding the run. Umpire Hank O'Day bore witness to the whole thing.

The score was therefore still tied at the end of nine innings, but with the field overrun with jubilant Giant fans (little did they know), the game was called. National League President Harry Pulliam upheld O'Day's action and the game was declared a tie. The significance of this grew to immense proportions when the Giants and Cubs ended the season in a tie with identical 98–55 records. The September 23 game had to be played off, at the Polo Grounds on October 8. Before a packed house of 35,000, the Cubs behind Three Finger Brown beat the Giants and Mathewson 4–2.

It was a heartbreaking loss for the Giants, and forever after Fred Merkle was to be known as "Bonehead." McGraw, however, vigorously defended his young ballplayer, saying that Fred had only been following common practice in not running all the way to second. Merkle went on to a fine 16-year career in the major leagues, all of it destined to be overshadowed by what occurred during those confused and confusing moments on the afternoon of September 23, 1908, at the Polo Grounds.

For the Giants, the loss dimmed the luster of Mathewson's greatest season, the twenty-nine-year-old pitching idol posting a 37–11 record, with a 1.43 earned-run average for 391 innings of work.

Again it was a pitcher's league, with the hurlers dominating to the extent of holding the hitters to a feeble .239 batting average, still the lowest mark ever in National League history. They could not stop the mighty Wagner, however, the Pittsburgh star winning another batting title, with a .354 mark.

In 1909 Wagner gunned his club to the pennant, helping Pittsburgh celebrate the opening of Forbes Field, a triple-decked steel ball park destined to be the home of the Pirates for more than 60 years. The Pirates won 110 games, still the second-highest total in National League history and pretty close to what they needed, the Cubs going down fighting, winning 104 games in their drive for a fourth-straight flag. Chance's team lost despite a collective 1.75 ERA, as he got superb seasons out of Brown, Overall, Reulbach, and Pfeister. Pittsburgh, however, got a 25–6 season from right-hander Howie Camnitz, while veteran Vic Willis won 20 for the eighth time in an outstanding career.

Frank Chance got his boys back on top for the fourth time in five years in 1910, winning 104 games and coasting in 13 ahead of the Giants. The Cubs got unexpected pitching help from rookie right-hander Leonard ("King") Cole, who broke in with a scintillating 20–4 record. The young man was going to have a brief and sad career. After two fine seasons with the Cubs, he was traded to the Pirates, pitched there and for the Yankees with modest success, and then in January 1916 died at the age of twenty-nine.

Batting averages jumped —the league batting .256, 12 points higher than the year before—and there was a reason for it. The A. J. Reach Company had patented a cork-center baseball with a bit more life in it, and this was reflected in batting averages as well as earned-run averages. The Cub pitchers again led the league, but this time with an ERA of 2.51.

It was in July 1910 that *New York Mail* columnist Franklin P. Adams published his poem that immortalized the Cubs' infield. After witnessing what must have been a pretty nifty double play, the dismayed but admiring Adams, a Giant fan, went home and wrote:

These are the saddest of possible words—
Tinker to Evers to Chance.
Trio of Bear Cubs and fleeter than birds—
Tinker to Evers to Chance.
Thoughtlessly pricking our gonfalon bubble,
Making a Giant hit into a double,
Words that are weighty with nothing but trouble,
Tinker to Evers to Chance.

Ed Delahanty, the National League's premier hitter with Philadelphia until defecting to Washington in the American League in 1902. A year later he died in a mysterious train accident at Niagara Falls, New York, at the age of thirty-five.

Wee Willie Keeler.

Jesse Burkett.

Bobby Wallace.

Fred Clarke, outfielder with Louisville and Pittsburgh from 1894 to 1915. His lifetime average: .315. Fred managed the club from 1897 to 1915.

Outfielder-third baseman Tommy Leach, one of the mainstays of the Pirate pennant-winning clubs early in the century. Tommy played from 1898 to 1918.

A lineup of derby-hatted spectators watching the Giants play from the bluff overlooking the Polo Grounds. The year is 1905.

Clarence ("Ginger") Beaumont, steady-hitting out-fielder with Pittsburgh, Boston, and Chicago from 1899 to 1910. Ginger led the league with a .357 average in 1902 and four times led in hits, finishing with a lifetime average of .311. Notice his glove—standard big-league equipment of the day.

Charles ("Deacon") Phillippe pitched for Louisville and Pittsburgh from 1899 to 1911, winning 20 or more his first five years in the league. His lifetime record: 186–109.

Sam Crawford, hard-hitting outfielder with Cincinnati at the turn of the century. Sam led the league with 16 home runs in 1901. In 1903 he jumped to the American League and had a long and brilliant career with Detroit.

Honus Wagner.

William ("Kitty") Bransfield, National League first baseman in 1898 and from 1901 to 1911. Kitty split his prime years between Pittsburgh and Philadelphia.

Jimmy Sheckard starred with Brooklyn and Chicago, among others, in a career that stretched from 1897 through 1913. Jimmy, an outfielder, led the league with 9 home runs in 1903. His 147 walks in 1911 stood as a league record until topped by Eddie Stanky's 148 in 1945.

Sam Leever, crack right-hander with Pittsburgh from 1898 to 1910. A four-time 20-game winner, Sam's top year was 1903, when he was 25–7 and led in winning percentage, earned-run average, and shutouts. Lifetime he was 194–100. For National League pitchers in the twentieth century, Sam's .660 lifetime winning percentage is second only to Mathewson's .665.

Right-hander Jack Taylor pitched for Chicago and St. Louis from 1898 to 1907, winning 20 or better four times. From 1902 through 1905 Jack started and completed 139 games, including a record 39 complete games in 1904.

A National Leaguer from 1895 to 1908, Dan McGann played first base for McGraw when the Giants took their first pennant in 1905.

Frank ("Noodles") Hahn, a quality left-hander with Cincinnati in the early days of the century. Noodles was 23–7 in his rookie year of 1899 and won over 20 three more times before finishing up with the Yankees in 1906.

James ("Cy") Seymour, outfielder with New York and Cincinnati from 1896 to 1910. Cy led in batting in 1905, with a .377 average, and also led in hits, doubles, triples, runs batted in, and slugging. Lifetime batting average: .303.

Luther ("Dummy") Taylor. Taylor, a deaf-mute, pitched for the Giants early in the century. His big year was 1904, when he was 27–15.

Charles ("Red") Dooin, National League catcher from 1902 to 1916, most of it spent with Philadelphia, where he also managed from 1910 to 1914.

Roger Bresnahan, McGraw's regular catcher in the first decade of the century. Roger, credited with being the first catcher to wear shin guards, played in the big leagues in 1897 and from 1900 to 1915, most of it spent in the National League with New York, St. Louis, and Chicago. He hit .350 in 1903 and has a .280 lifetime batting average.

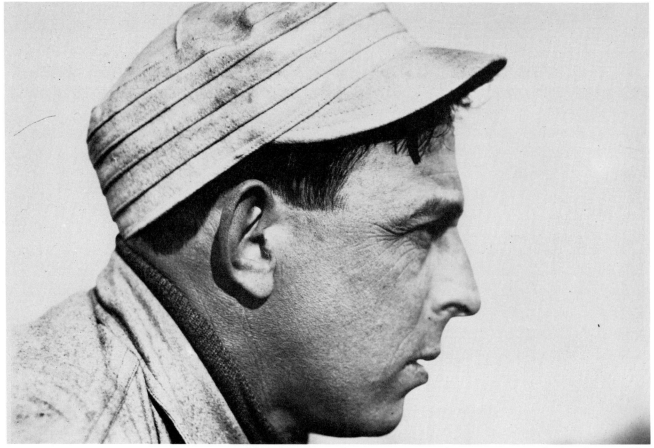

A big leaguer from 1896 to 1906, outfielder Sam Mertes spent some productive years with the Giants. His 104 RBIs led the league in 1903.

Bob Ewing, National League pitcher from 1902 to 1912, mostly with Cincinnati. With a lifetime record of 123–119, Bob's best year was 1905, when he was 20–11.

Jake Weimer, a left-hander who pitched for the Cubs and Reds from 1903 to 1908. Jake broke in with 21–9 and 20–14 seasons for Chicago.

"Iron Man" Joe McGinnity, ace big-league pitcher from 1899 to 1908. Joe won 31 for McGraw in 1903 and was even better the next year, when he was 35–8. Lifetime Joe was 247–145.

Christy Mathewson in 1906.

Art Devlin, a rugged character, was McGraw's third baseman from 1904 to 1911 before joining the Braves for two years. He was the stolen base champ in 1905 with 59.

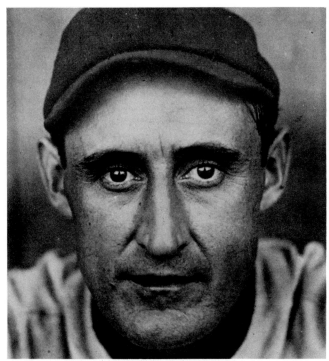

George ("Hooks") Wiltse. This wily lefty was a steady winner for the Giants from 1904 to 1914, winning 23 in 1908 and 20 a year later. Lifetime he stands at 141–90.

Mickey Doolin, a big leaguer from 1905 to 1918; from 1905 to 1913 the Phillies' regular shortstop.

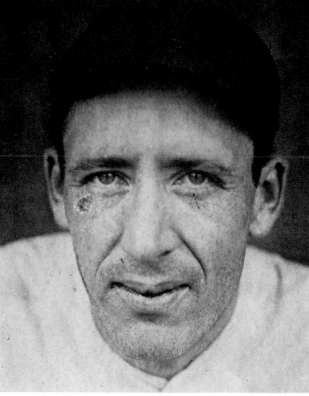

Harry Lumley, Brooklyn outfielder from 1904 to 1910, was one of the club's stronger hitters. In his rookie year he led the league with 9 home runs and 18 triples.

Leon ("Red") Ames, a right-hander who worked the National League mounds from 1903 to 1919. Pitching for New York, Cincinnati, St. Louis, and Philadelphia, Ames logged a 183–167 lifetime record, with a 22–8 season for the Giants in 1905 his best showing.

Harry Steinfeldt, a solid third baseman with Cincinnati, Chicago, and Boston in the National League from 1898 to 1911. His best year was 1906 when he batted .327.

Mordecai ("Three Finger") Brown. Brown was a six-time 20-game winner, with highs of 29 in 1908 and 27 in 1909. From 1906 through 1909 his record was 102–30. He pitched in the National League for 12 years, retiring with a lifetime 208–111 record.

Ed Reulbach. Ed pitched at the top from 1905 through 1917, with one year out for the Federal League. His great years were with the Cubs. In 1906 he was 20–4, in 1908 24–7. Lifetime his record is an impressive 165–94.

Jack Pfeister. Frank Chance's lefty ace pitched in the big leagues from 1903 through 1911. In 1906 he was 19–9; a year later he was the ERA leader with a 1.15 mark.

Johnny Evers (left) and Frank Chance (right). The man in the middle is Barney Oldfield, the top racing car driver of the day.

Joe Tinker. The front man on baseball's most famous double-play combination, Joe played in the big leagues from 1902 through 1916, most of it with the Cubs.

Frank ("Wildfire") Schulte obliging the photographer at the batting cage in 1910. Frank, who led the league in home runs in 1910 and 1911, played in the big leagues from 1904 through 1918, the first 13 of those years with the Cubs.

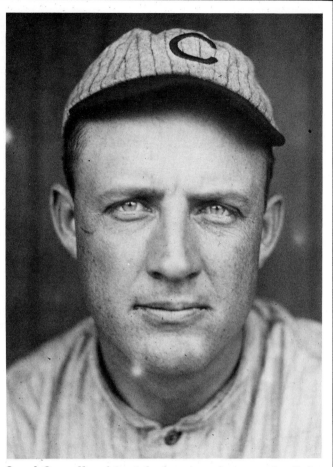

Solly Hofman, one of the key men on the fine Cub pennant winners of 1906–1908. An outfielder who came to the league in 1903, Solly's best year was 1910, when he batted .325.

Orval Overall, a big right-hander who gave the Cubs 20-game seasons in 1907 and 1909. His 23 wins in 1907 were tops in the league.

Johnny Kling, one of the great catchers of his time. Johnny got to the big time with the Cubs in 1900. He was traded to the Braves in 1911 and finished out with the Reds in 1913.

You're looking at a two-time home run champion. Brooklyn first baseman Tim Jordan led the National League with 12 homers in 1906 and again with 12 in 1908. Two years later an injury brought Tim's career to a premature end.

George Gibson came up with Pittsburgh in 1905 and did the bulk of the catching until 1916, when he was dealt to the Giants.

Christy Mathewson.

Albert ("Lefty") Leifield, a 21-game winner with the Pirates in 1907. Lefty pitched in the National League, with the Pirates and Cubs, from 1905 to 1913.

Pittsburgh's Vic Willis, one of the great pitchers of the time, is shown warming up at the Pirates' Exposition Park, forerunner of Forbes Field. Willis entered the National League with Boston in 1898, joined the Pirates in 1906, and finished with St. Louis in 1910. Vic won 20 or better eight times and has a lifetime record of 248–208.

John ("Hans") Lobert, a swift little third baseman who played for Pittsburgh, Chicago, Cincinnati, Philadelphia, and New York from 1903 to 1917.

First baseman Ed Konetchy. Ed came to the big leagues with the Cardinals in 1907 and later played for Pittsburgh, Boston, Brooklyn, and Cincinnati.

At bat at the Polo Grounds in 1909 is Al Bridwell, the man whose line shot sent Fred Merkle on his fateful, uncompleted journey. Al was a National League shortstop with four clubs from 1905 to 1913.

Right-hander Nick Maddox had a brief but very successful career with the Pirates from 1907 to 1910. Nick was 23–8 in 1908.

Fred Merkle, a fine major-league first baseman for 15 years, but destined to be always remembered for one base-running lapse.

George McQuillan, a right-handed pitcher, came to the National League with the Phillies in 1907. A year later he had his biggest season, winning 23 and losing 17.

Harry Coveleski had his big years with Detroit around the time of the world war, but he came up with the Phillies in 1907 and had some fair success until the Phillies let him get away.

Charles ("Babe") Adams, one of Pittsburgh's all-time pitching greats. Adams, a righty, worked for the Pirates from 1907 through 1926. His lifetime record was 194–140, with 22 wins in 1911 his best total. A control artist, Babe walked just 430 batters in nearly 3,000 innings.

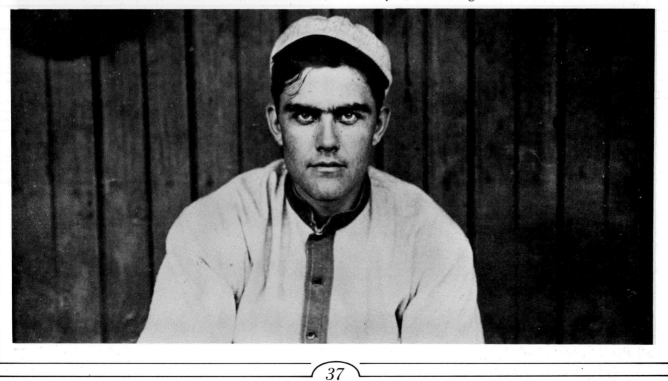

George ("Dode") Paskert, outfielder with the Reds, Phillies, and Cubs between 1907 and 1921.

Howie Camnitz. Howie joined the Pirates in 1904 and hit his stride in 1909 with a 25–6 record. He was a 20-game winner again in 1911 and 1912. In 1914 he jumped to the Federal League and finished his career there.

John McGraw hitting grounders to his infield in pregame practice. (Managers worked harder in those years.) Standing behind him is catcher Chief Meyers. The year is 1910.

Jimmy Archer, Chicago Cubs catcher from 1909 to 1917.

Earl Moore joined the Phillies in 1908 after seven years in the American League. He was a 21-game winner in 1910.

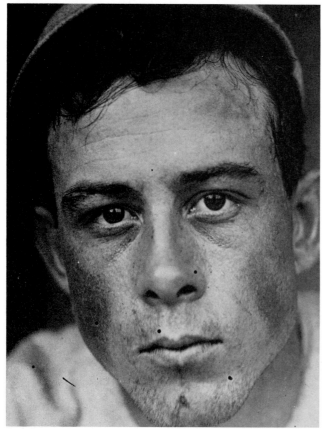

Catcher Bill Rariden as a rookie with the Braves in 1909. Bill later caught for the Giants and Reds, retiring in 1920.

Arthur ("Bugs") Raymond (right), a talented pitcher for the Cardinals and Giants between 1907 and 1911. Bugs might have lasted longer, except for a weakness for the bottle. He drank himself out of the big leagues in 1911 and a year later died at the age of thirty.

Bob Bescher, outfielder and base-stealing special-ist. Bob played with the Reds, Giants, and Cardi-nals from 1908 to 1917. He led the league in stolen bases four straight times, from 1909 to 1912, with a peak of 80 in 1911, a National League record that stood until Maury Wills broke it in 1962.

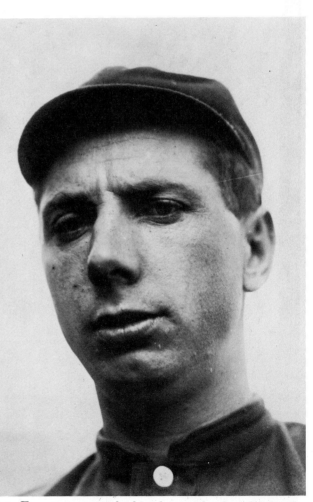

Art Fromme, a right-hander with the Cardinals, Reds, and Giants from 1906 to 1915. He won 19 for the Reds in 1909.

Pitcher George Suggs worked for the Reds from 1910 to 1913. He turned in 19 wins for the Reds in 1912.

Rogers Hornsby. Lifetime average: .358.

John McGraw and Others

The next three years belonged to John McGraw and his New York Giants. With the incomparable Mathewson winning 26, 23, and 25, and teaming with a tall left-handed fireballer named Rube Marquard, who had win totals of 24, 26, and 23, the Giants took pennants in 1911, 1912, and 1913. In 1911 McGraw's boys stole 347 bases, still the major-league record. A year later they slowed down to 319, and the next year 296. These were mighty Giant teams, leading the league in stolen bases and batting average in each of those pennant years.

For Marquard, the Giants had paid the Indianapolis club $11,000 in 1908. It was a considerable sum of money for the time and when Rube broke in with two mediocre years, he became dubbed the "eleven-thousand-dollar lemon." But Rube then proved out, particularly in 1912, when he won 19 consecutive games.

Years later, when he was just breaking into the league in 1930, Al Lopez remembered what a McGraw team looked like on the field: "When they threw the ball around during infield practice, they really fired it; that's the way he wanted them to do it. When you watched that Giant team on the field, you could always feel McGraw's hand everywhere. He was all business on a ball field, and so were they." So it was in 1930 and so it always was with a McGraw team. His players were well paid, and he instilled in them the same pride in being Giants that Yankee players were to feel decades later when drawing on their pinstripes.

The 1911–1913 winners were a fairly set team, with Fred Merkle, Larry Doyle, Art Fletcher, and Buck Herzog in the infield; Chief Meyers catching;

Red Murray, Fred Snodgrass, Josh Devore, and George Burns in the outfield. It was a team geared for a slashing, daring offensive game. In the three pennant-winning years Meyers batted .332, .358, and .312, with the .358 mark the highest ever recorded by a National League catcher. McGraw's second baseman, "Laughing Larry" Doyle, a spirited, hard-playing youngster filled with the joy of youth and the brimming abundance of his talent, coined one of the loveliest of all baseball lines when he said, "It's great to be young and a Giant."

In 1911 Chicago's Frank Schulte, nicknamed "Wildfire," did some heroic slugging, setting a new major-league home run record with 21 round trippers, breaking Sam Crawford's mark of 16, set ten years before. There was more and more hitting now, with the league climbing to a .260 batting average. Only one earned-run average under 2.00 was recorded that year, and fittingly it belonged to Mathewson—1.99.

The top pitchers were still working well— New York's Mathewson, Chicago's Three Finger Brown, Brooklyn's fine lefty Nap Rucker. But the outstanding pitcher in the league in 1911, and for years to come, was a lanky, freckle-faced, easygoing right-handed rookie with the Phillies named Grover Cleveland Alexander.

"If there was ever a better pitcher than Alexander," said Burleigh Grimes years later, "I never saw him." Alex had everything—speed, an assortment of curves, and control. His story is truly one of triumph and tragedy. He scaled heights where only Mathewson's footprints lay imprinted, then suffered a fall from grace worthy of Greek tragedy. After service in World War I, during which he endured some brutal artillery bombardments, Alex became an alcoholic and began suffering from epileptic seizures. His dazzling natural ability sustained him for years; but when time and whiskey finally took their toll, Alex's descent was precipitous and pathetic. His most indel-

ible moment came in the 1926 World Series against the Yankees, when the thirty-nine-year-old veteran fanned rookie slugger Tony Lazzeri with the bases loaded in the seventh inning of the seventh game, setting the stage for a world championship.

In 1911 the world belonged to Alexander. Working for a fourth-place Philadelphia team, the rookie won an astounding 28 games, lost 13, led with 7 shutouts, 31 complete games, and fanned 227, still the league record for a first-year man.

Alex slipped to a 19–17 season in 1912, pitching for a fifth-place club. If there had been a Most Valuable Player Award at that time, it would probably have gone to Chicago's Heinie Zimmerman. The Cub third baseman led the league with a .372 batting average, 14 home runs, 42 doubles, and 207 hits. There was, in fact, a forerunner of the MVP awards at the time, called the Chalmers Award, named for the automobile manufacturer that donated one of its cars to the best player in each league. The awards were in effect for only four years, 1911 through 1914. The winners were Wildfire Schulte, Larry Doyle (over Zimmerman in 1912), Brooklyn's Jake Daubert, and Johnny Evers in 1914, Johnny then playing for Boston.

Evers' award in 1914 indicates what a spark plug Johnny must have been on the diamond, what non-box-score intangibles he must have brought to his game, for the little second baseman batted only .279 and led in no offensive categories. One of his contemporaries said of Johnny that "he excited a ball game." Well, Johnny and his teammates "excited" a lot of ball games in 1914; so many, in fact, that they wrought a "miracle."

As late as July 19 the Boston Braves were in last place. But then the team got hot and stayed hot. On August 10 they were second, and on September 8 they took over first place and stayed there. The Braves never did cool off; for once they clinched the pennant they kept on winning, ending up 10½ games ahead of the Giants. They made the miracle all the more genuine by then sweeping the World Series against a powerful and highly favored Philadelphia Athletics team.

The miracle was wrought by some flashy infield play by veteran second baseman Evers and a young shortstop named Walter ("Rabbit") Maranville, playing his third season in the big leagues (he would put in another 20). Manager George Stallings' team had three strong pitchers—Dick Rudolph, Bill James, and Lefty Tyler. Rudolph and James won 27 and 26 games respectively and Tyler 16. The three stalwarts started 107 of the Braves' games in 1914.

War broke out in Europe in 1914 and baseball went through a battle of its own. A third major league, the Federal League, set up shop that year. With teams in Pittsburgh, St. Louis, Kansas City, Brooklyn, Buffalo, Indianapolis, Chicago, and Baltimore, the newcomers were supplied with fresh bankrolls and enticing checkbooks. It was the old story all over again, with players jumping from one league to another.

The National League was hit harder than the American, losing top names like Joe Tinker, Three Finger Brown, Howie Camnitz, Claude Hendrix, Ed Reulbach, Lee Magee, and Tom Seaton, a 27-game winner for the Phillies in 1913.

The Federal League was destined to last only two years. Lawsuits began piling up, while attendance fell short of hopes and expectations. Peace was made after the 1915 season and the new league disbanded. One player developed by the Feds, outfielder Edd Roush, joined the Giants in 1916, was traded to Cincinnati, and went on to become one of the National League's greatest outfielders. Roush was a tough-minded, independent young man and he refused to knuckle under to McGraw. Getting rid of Roush was probably the biggest trading mistake the Giant manager ever made.

Going to Cincinnati with Roush was Christy Mathewson. The thirty-six-year-old Matty had finally shown signs of mortality in 1915, finishing the season with an 8–14 record, and a year later, when offered the opportunity of managing the Reds, Christy was given his chance by McGraw. Mathewson managed Cincinnati for two and a half years, leaving after a third-place finish in 1918 to enlist in the army. When he left the service he returned to the Giants and for three years served as a coach under McGraw.

In 1915 Grover Cleveland Alexander became without peer among National League pitchers, reaching the heights with a 31–10 mark. The twenty-eight-year-old right-hander delivered 12 shutouts and posted a stunning 1.22 earned-run average, all the more remarkable because he was pitching half his games in a bandbox called Baker Bowl, a ball park whose beckoning right-field wall made healthy pitchers ill and ailing batters well.

In hurling the Phillies to their first pennant in 1915, Alex was abetted by the record-breaking home run bat of outfielder Gavvy Cravath. This muscleman, baseball's premier long baller before Babe Ruth, broke Schulte's mark with 24 home runs. Otherwise, it was far from a banner year for National League hitters, with New York's Larry Doyle taking the batting title with a .320 average, still the lowest ever for a titlist in the league. The year also saw the great man himself, John J. McGraw, suffer the embarrassment of his one and only last-place finish. It was true that McGraw's 69–83 record left him only 3½ games out of fourth place, but that can hardly have helped his already grainy disposition.

If National League hitting had become feeble, then the St. Louis Cardinals were about to do their bit to help change that. The club in 1915 introduced to the league a nineteen-year-old infielder who would soon become its all-time smasher. He was a cold-eyed Texan named Rogers Hornsby, a right-handed hitter with a picture-perfect swing and a personality as sharp and singular as the line drives he rifled in all directions. The young man's debut was modest: in 18 games he batted just .246. But for National League pitchers it was a case of bad news slipping in quietly in the night.

In 1916, for the third year in a row, a National League team won its first pennant. This time it was the Brooklyn Dodgers, a club that eventually grew into the league's most colorful and fabled franchise. Playing their fourth season in their impressive new ball park, Ebbets Field (named for their owner), the Dodgers finally won one. Their manager was portly Wilbert Robinson, formerly a catcher and teammate of McGraw's on the Baltimore Orioles clubs of the 1890s, in the early decades of the century still the touchstone of team greatness. Uncle Robbie, as people came to call him, was a lovable bumbler of a manager, a fine handler of pitchers but also somewhat absentminded. Before taking over the Dodgers in 1914, Robbie had been coaching for his old buddy McGraw, but the two friends came to a bitter parting of the ways and Robinson headed for Brooklyn, where he remained until 1931.

The Dodgers always seemed to draw vivid characters to their roster, and in 1916 the cast included a twenty-five-year-old outfielder named Casey Stengel. The irrepressible Stengel personality, which New York fans came to know and appreciate years later when he was managing the Yankees, was in evidence as long ago as 1916. Before the first game of the World Series, Stengel approached several members of the highly favored Red Sox on the field and said, "Tell me, boys—what do you think our loser's share will come to?" (Casey knew whereof he spoke; the Dodgers went down in five.)

Helping the Dodgers to the pennant were ex-Giants Marquard, Merkle, and Meyers. It was a rebuilding year for McGraw's club, which finished fourth that year despite an astonishing 26-game winning streak in September, all the wins coming at home.

Alexander helped the Phillies make a race of it, winning 33 games as his club fell 2½ games short of Brooklyn at the end of the season. Among Alex's achievements this year were an all-time record 16 shutouts, 9 of them in Baker Bowl. In St. Louis, young Hornsby, dividing his time between third base and shortstop in his first full season, batted .313. It was the first rumble of this particular thunder coming out of the West.

In 1917 John McGraw completed the journey from last place to first in two years, easily outlegging the second-place Phillies by ten games. Alexander again dominated the league's pitching with a 30–13 mark, equaling Mathewson's record of three consecutive 30-game seasons. The year marked the end of the road for Pittsburgh's incomparable Honus Wagner. At the age of forty-three the Flying Dutchman got into 74 games, most of them at first base, and batted .265. When all accounts were in, Wagner had accumulated 3,430 hits, a league record that stood until 1962, when Stan Musial finally shot it down.

One of the memorable games in baseball history was played on May 2, 1917, in Chicago between the Cubs and Reds. The Cubs' left-hander Jim ("Hippo") Vaughan and the Reds' Fred Toney hooked up in the only double no-hit game ever in the major leagues. The scoreless, hitless game went into the tenth inning, when the Reds made two hits off of Vaughan and scored a run. Toney maintained his mastery in the bottom of the tenth and completed his no-hitter.

In 1918 baseball began feeling the heat of the war, which America had entered in 1917. Big-league rosters began being depleted by players going off to the armed forces, either as draftees or as volunteers. In June, the government issued a "work-or-fight" order, with draft-age men forced into a choice between the military and essential industries. Baseball was classified as nonessential. The game was given a grace period in which to complete its schedule, with Labor Day being designated as the season's end.

Among the National Leaguers who went off to fight in "the war to end all wars" were Casey Stengel, Jeff Pfeffer, Rube Benton, Bill James, Rabbit Maranville, Hank Gowdy (the first to enlist), Eddie Grant (killed in action in France), Eppa Rixey, and Grover Cleveland Alexander. When Alex left early in the 1918 season, it was a Chicago Cub uniform he peeled off. The Phillies, sensing that their great pitcher might be drafted, had dealt him to the Cubs the previous November for two players and $60,000. The Phillies were correct, but it was this kind of wrongheaded thinking that dumped the team into the cellar for most of the next decade and a half, since Alex came back from the wars a little the worse for wear but still a winning pitcher for another decade.

The abbreviated 1918 season pennant winners were the Cubs, led by Hippo Vaughan's 22 wins.

When the war ended in November 1918, the lords of baseball were uncertain about the direction the national economy was heading. Consequently, they scheduled a 140-game season. But baseball's fears about the economy were ill-founded. The nation was heading into the most tumultuous, prosperous, and free-spending decade in its history. The passion for baseball was never more in evidence. Major-league attendance was up dramatically at every port of call; in Brooklyn it was quadrupled, in Cincinnati more than tripled, while the Giants jumped from 250,000 turnstile spins to more than 700,000.

In 1919 the Reds, led by their batting champion center fielder Edd Roush, won their first pennant, finishing a comfortable nine games ahead of the Giants. Cincinnati then went on to take the World Series from the Chicago White Sox, one of the greatest teams of all time. To close observers, the White Sox's performance left behind an unpleasant odor. Something seemed wrong. And something had indeed been wrong: in September 1920 eight members of the White Sox were accused of accepting bribes to throw the series.

It was baseball's most sordid era, a time when the public came dangerously close to losing faith in its national game. The "Black Sox scandal," as the affair became known, overshadowed similar shenanigans, some of which had evidently been going on for some time. In 1919 two of McGraw's stars, brilliant but unscrupulous first baseman Hal Chase and third baseman Heinie Zimmerman, were barred from professional baseball forever for trying to induce players to throw games. A year later Chicago's Lee Magee was sent packing for the same reason.

In order to restore the public's trust and confidence in the integrity of the game, baseball hired a federal judge with the resounding name of Kenesaw Mountain Landis as commissioner, vested him with sweeping dictatorial powers, and charged him with cleaning up the game. Landis signed a seven-year contract at a reported $50,000 a year. The judge remained on the job until his death in 1944 at the age of seventy-eight.

Landis served notice immediately that he was going to be an unforgiving arbiter of the game's ethics when he declared ineligible forever the eight White Sox players along with Chase, Zimmerman, Magee, and several others who had dared sully the game's good name.

The league went back to a 154-game schedule in 1920 and the Dodgers won their second pennant. Wilbert Robinson got 23 wins out of his tough, hard-boiled spitballer Burleigh Grimes and a sharp-hitting season from veteran outfielder Zack Wheat, Brooklyn's first baseball hero. McGraw's Giants, despite 20-game seasons from Fred Toney, Art Nehf, and Jesse Barnes, finished second, seven games out.

The season was marked by one of those oddball games with which the Dodgers soon came to be associated. On May 1 a pair of right-handers, Brooklyn's Leon Cadore and Boston's Joe Oeschger, matched off in a 26-

inning 1–1 tie that was finally halted by darkness, both pitchers going all the way. The game remains the standard for longevity, and Oeschger and Cadore have become inseparably linked in baseball lore like Tinker, Evers, and Chance, and Ruth and Gehrig, and Branca and Thomson.

With the advent of the lively ball and the large crowds drawn by Babe Ruth's distance hitting, the owners decided to turn the game more in the direction of the hitters. Consequently, all trick pitches, most prominently the spitball, were outlawed. Those pitchers who used a wet one as their primary weapon were allowed to continue employing it; for others it was strictly illegal, with a ten-day suspension awaiting any who tried. Among the sanctioned spitballers were the Cardinals' Bill Doak, the Giants' Phil Douglas, and the most famous baseball moistener of the time, Brooklyn's Burleigh Grimes. Grimes, who pitched in the big leagues until 1934, was the last of the legal spitball pitchers. The illegal variety, however, continue to flourish.

Although there were no Babe Ruths in the National League—Philadelphia's Cy Williams won the home run crown with 15 (Ruth tagged an awesome 54 for the Yankees, more than any National League team except the Phillies)—there was a Rogers Hornsby. The Cardinals' second baseman took the first of six consecutive batting championships with a .370 mark, a hefty figure but low by the standards Hornsby was about to set. Led by this Texan with the gunfighters' cold gray eyes, the National League's greatest decade of hitting had begun.

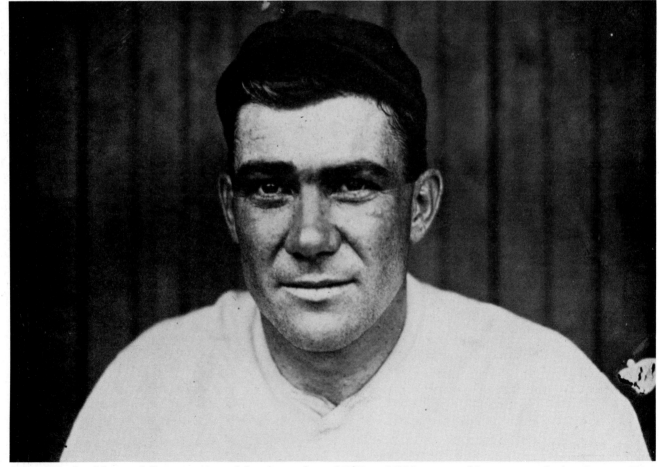

Larry Doyle, National League second baseman from 1907 to 1920, most of it spent with the Giants. Five times a .300 hitter, "Laughing Larry" led the league with a .320 average in 1915.

Josh Devore, one of McGraw's speedy outfielders. Josh played from 1908 to 1913.

John ("Red") Murray. Red came up with the Cardinals in 1906 and was traded to the Giants in 1909, for whom he put in his best years. His modest seven home runs led the league in 1909. Red played until 1917.

Chief Meyers shaping up the infield before a 1912 World Series game with the Red Sox at the Polo Grounds. John McGraw is making sure it's done right.

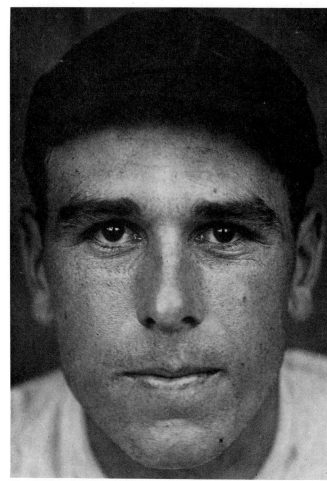

Fred Snodgrass, National League outfielder from 1908 to 1916, most of it spent in a Giant uniform. Fred gave McGraw a .321 year in 1910.

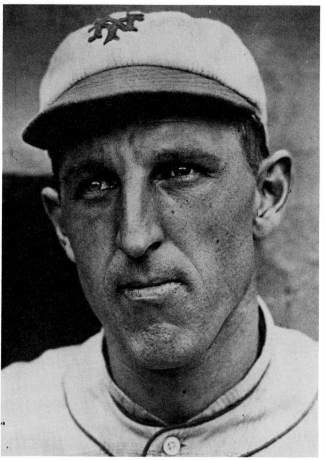

Charles ("Buck") Herzog. Buck played from 1908 to 1920. McGraw didn't like him personally but admired Buck's infield play. Consequently, John J. dealt him away three times and reacquired him twice.

Otis ("Doc") Crandall, a steady right-hander who pitched for McGraw from 1908 to 1913. His top year was 1910, when he was 17–4. Doc could swing the bat, too, and was often used as a pinch hitter.

Art Fletcher, McGraw's hard-playing shortstop from 1909 to 1920.

Rube Marquard. From 1911 to 1913 Rube won 24, 26 and 23 games. He pitched from 1908 to 1925 and overall won 204 games.

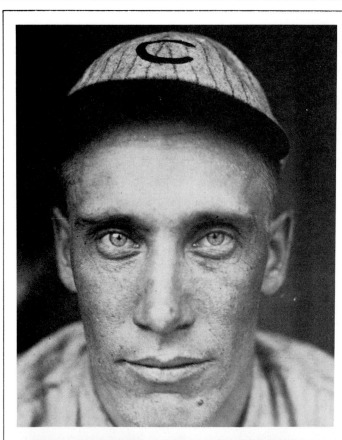

Leonard ("King") Cole, a 20-game winner with the Cubs in 1910.

"Turkey" Mike Donlin. Mike bounced around the league with the Cardinals, Giants, Reds, Braves, and Pirates, hitting .300 wherever he went. He peaked with McGraw in 1905 with a .356 average. Mike played from 1899 to 1914, hitting over .300 ten times. He left baseball at the age of thirty-six to go into vaudeville. Above, he is receiving a gold bat at the Polo Grounds in 1911. On the left are Giant teammates George Burns, Hooks Wiltse, and Christy Mathewson.

Vic Saier, Cub first baseman from 1911 to 1917.

Henry (Heinie) Zimmerman, infielder with the Cubs from 1907 to 1916, then with the Giants until 1919.

Larry Cheney, a right-handed spitballer who joined the Cubs in 1911. In 1912 he was a 26-game winner, then won 20 in each of the next two seasons.

Fred Luderus. He came up as a first baseman with the Cubs in 1909, but from 1910 through 1920 handled the position for the Phillies.

Bill McKechnie came to the National League as an infielder with the Pirates in 1907. No great shakes as a player, he went on to become a pennant-winning manager with Pittsburgh, St. Louis, and Cincinnati.

Grover Cleveland Alexander. His 373 lifetime victories tie him with Mathewson as the league's all-time leader.

Nap Rucker, probably the greatest left-hander ever to pitch for the Brooklyn Dodgers. Nap's lifetime ERA for a career that went from 1907 through 1916 was 2.42.

Grover Cleveland Alexander.

Eddie Grant, third baseman with the Phillies, Reds, and Giants from 1907 to 1915. Eddie enlisted in the infantry in World War I. He was killed in France a month before the armistice was signed.

Right-hander Bob Harmon pitched for the Cardinals and Pirates from 1909 through 1918, with a 23–15 mark in 1911 his best effort.

George Burns, another of McGraw's base-path flashes. George, an outfielder, played in the National League from 1911 through 1925, the first 11 of those years with the Giants. George led in stolen bases twice and runs scored five times.

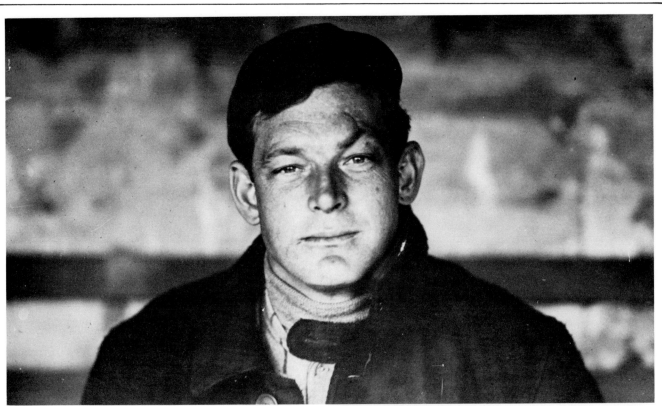

Charles ("Jeff") Tesreau, one of McGraw's aces from 1912 to 1918. The right-hander led in ERA (1.96) in his rookie year, then won 22 in 1913 and a career-high 26 in 1914.

One of the most popular of all Brooklyn players, Zack Wheat played for the Dodgers from 1909 to 1926. He batted .375 in 1923 and again the next year. His lifetime batting average is .317.

This gentleman owns what is probably one of the game's unbreakable hitting records. His name is Owen Wilson. In 1912, while playing for the Pirates, he hit an incredible 36 triples. Wilson played for Pittsburgh from 1908 through 1913, and for St. Louis from 1914 through 1916.

Claude Hendrix came up with the Pirates in 1911 and had his biggest year in 1912, when he was 23–9. He later pitched for the Cubs, retiring in 1920.

Jimmy Lavender, pitcher for the Cubs from 1912 through 1916 and then with the Phillies in 1917.

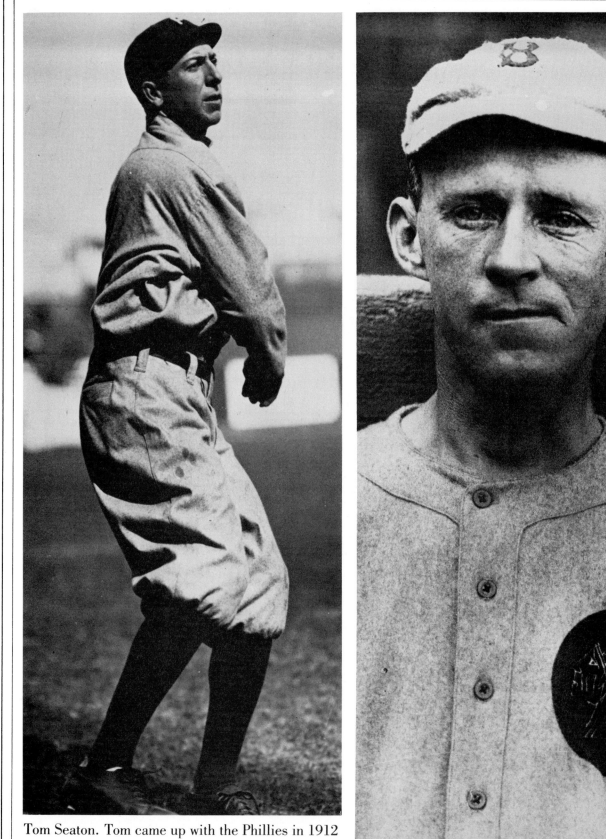

Tom Seaton. Tom came up with the Phillies in 1912 and a year later was 27–12. He spent the next two years in the Federal League, then finished up with the Cubs in 1917, never having regained his early, spectacular touch.

Johnny Evers with the "miracle" Braves in 1914.

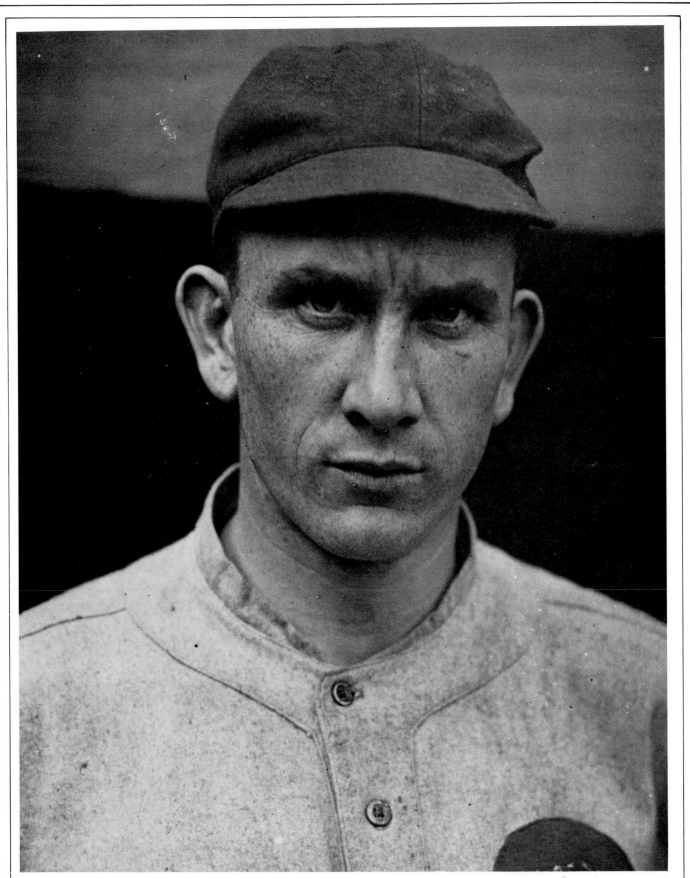

Walter ("Rabbit") Maranville, who played more games at shortstop (2,153) than any man in National League history. Rabbit came to the bigs with the Braves in 1912, later played for the Pirates, Cubs, Dodgers, Cardinals, and finished with the Braves in 1935.

Bill James joined the Braves in 1913, had one big year in 1914, when he won 26 and lost 7 for the "miracle" team, suffered an arm injury, and quickly faded from the scene.

Dick Rudolph, a 27-game winner for the 1914 Braves. The right-hander pitched from 1910 through 1920, with scattered appearances in later years. Lifetime record: 121–108.

George ("Lefty") Tyler. Lefty came up with the Braves in 1910 and finished up with the Cubs in 1921. He was 16–14 in the "miracle" year, 125–119 lifetime.

Hank Gowdy, catcher for the 1914 Braves. Hank came up in 1910 and caught for 17 years.

Clifford ("Gavvy") Cravath, the league's big home run hitter of the World War I era. Gavvy joined the Phillies in 1912 and played until 1920, leading in home runs six times, runs batted in twice. His 24 home runs in 1915 set a post-1900 major-league record. His lifetime average is .287.

Bill Killefer. "Reindeer Bill" joined the Phillies in 1911 and caught Grover Cleveland Alexander until 1917, when both were dealt to the Cubs. Bill remained with the Cubs until 1921.

Tom Hughes, a right-hander who had two good years with the Braves in 1915 and 1916, when he was 20–14 and 16–3.

Pat Moran, catcher with the Braves, Cubs, and Phillies from 1901 through 1914. In 1915 Pat managed the Phillies to their first pennant.

"Gentleman" Jake Daubert, talented Brooklyn first baseman from 1910 through 1918, then with Cincinnati until 1924. Jake took back-to-back batting titles in 1913 and 1914 with marks of .350 and .329. Ten times a .300 hitter, his lifetime average is .303.

Erskine Mayer, a right-hander who pitched for the Phillies and Pirates from 1912 through 1919. He was 21–19 with Philadelphia in 1914 and 21–15 the next year.

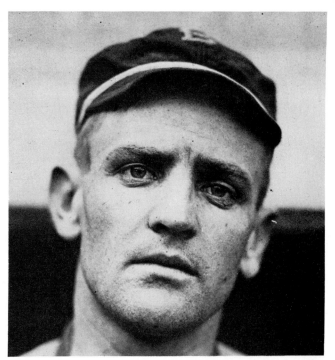

This young face belongs to Casey Stengel, rookie outfielder with the Dodgers in 1912. Stengel later played for the Pirates, Phillies, Giants, and Braves, retiring as a player in 1925. His lifetime average is .284.

Eppa Rixey, shown here as a Phillie rookie in 1912. The big left-hander pitched for Philadelphia until 1920, then went to Cincinnati, where he pursued his Hall of Fame career until 1933. Four times a 20-game winner, he reached his peak with a 25–13 record in 1922. Lifetime record: 266–251.

A one-time 30-game winner for the Philadelphia Athletics, right-hander Jack Coombs joined the Dodgers in 1915 and pitched for the Brooks for four years.

Wilbert Robinson, Dodger manager from 1914 through 1931.

Edward ("Jeff") Pfeffer, Dodger ace of the World War I era. Jeff won 23 in 1914 and 25 in 1916. He later pitched for the Cardinals and Pirates, winning 158 and losing 112 in a career that ran from 1913 through 1924.

Al Mamaux, right-hander with Pittsburgh from 1913 to 1917, then with Brooklyn from 1918 to 1923. Al's best years were 1915 and 1916, when he was 21–8 and 21–15.

Bill Hinchman, Pirate outfielder from 1915 to 1920.

"Spittin'" Bill Doak, who threw a wet one for the Reds, Cardinals, and Dodgers from 1912 through 1929. Bill won 20 for the Cards in 1914 and again in 1920. He was the ERA leader in 1914 and 1921. Lifetime record: 170–157.

Henry ("Heinie") Groh, sharp-hitting third baseman with the Reds, Giants, and Pirates from 1912 through 1927. His top year was 1921, when he batted .331 for the Reds. Lifetime average: .292.

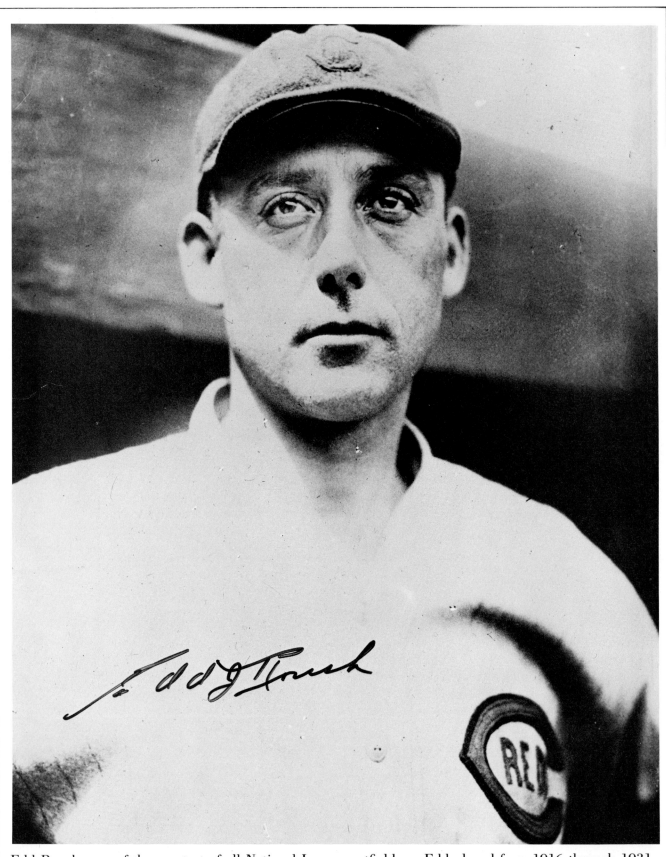

Edd Roush, one of the greatest of all National League outfielders. Edd played from 1916 through 1931, skipping the 1930 season as one of the game's first holdouts. Playing for Cincinnati from 1917 to 1926, Roush never batted under .321. He won batting titles in 1917 and 1919. Twelve times a .300 hitter, his lifetime average is .323.

Max Flack, outfielder with the Cubs and Cardinals from 1916 through 1925.

Al Demaree, a right-hander who pitched for the Giants, Phillies, Cubs, and Braves from 1912 through 1919. His best was a 19–14 season for the Phillies in 1916.

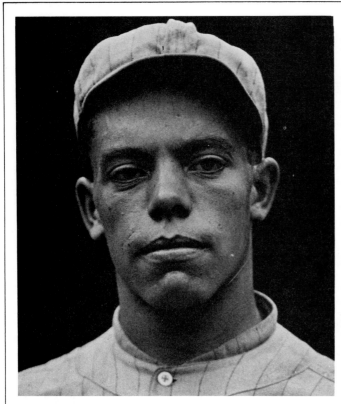

Left-hander Ferdie Schupp, National League pitcher from 1913 to 1921 with the Giants, Cardinals, and Dodgers. He gave McGraw his best year in 1917, when he was 21–7.

John ("Rube") Benton. Rube, a lefty, pitched in the National League from 1910 through 1925 with the Reds and Giants. His lifetime record is 155–144.

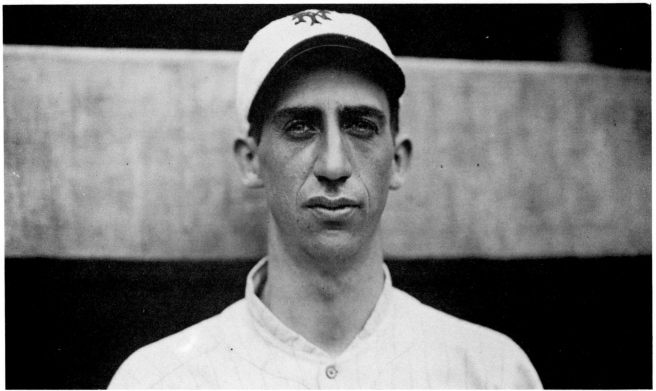

William ("Pol") Perritt. Perritt came to the majors with the Cardinals in 1912, moved over to the Giants in 1915, and won steadily for McGraw until stopped by a sore arm in 1919. The right-hander's best year was 1918, when he was 18–13.

After failing to make the grade with
the Yankees and Senators in the
American League, Jim ("Hippo")
Vaughan joined the Cubs in 1913
and made it big. Four times a 20-
game winner, with a peak of 23
in 1917, Vaughan's most memorable game was his double no-hit encounter with Fred Toney in 1917.
Vaughan retired in 1921 with a record of 176–137.

Fred Toney came up with the Cubs in 1911 and pitched for four clubs in a National League career that ran from 1911 through 1923. In 1917, the year he defeated Vaughan in their double no-hit encounter, Fred won 24 for the Reds. He was a 21-game winner for the Giants in 1920. Lifetime record: 137–102.

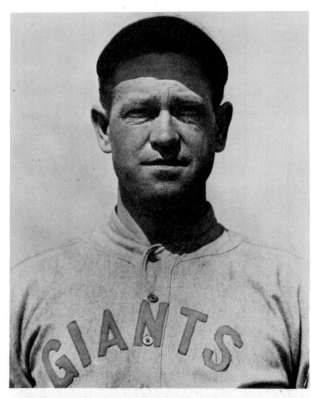

Hal Chase, peerless defensive first baseman and shady character. After 11 years in the American and Federal leagues, Hal joined the Reds in 1916 and led the league with a .339 average. He played for the Giants in 1919 before being barred from organized ball.

Walter Holke, first baseman who put in time with the Giants, Braves, Phillies, and Reds from 1914 through 1925.

Phil Douglas. They called him "Shufflin' Phil" and he shuffled through the league with the Reds, Dodgers, Cubs, and Giants between 1914 and 1922.

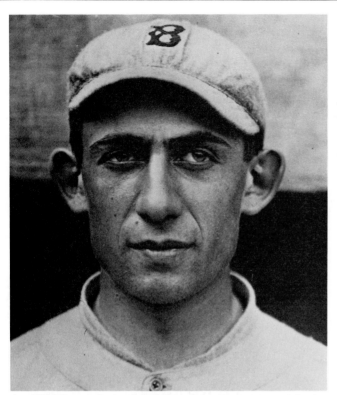

Art Nehf, a talented left-hander, came up with the Braves in 1915 and was traded to the Giants four years later. Art was a 20-game winner for McGraw in 1920–1921. He pitched in the National League until 1929, winning 184 and losing 120.

Carson Bigbee, outfielder with the Pirates from 1916 through 1926. Carson batted .350 in 1922 and had a lifetime average of .287.

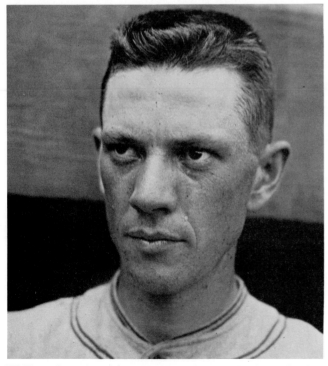

Wilbur Cooper, a gifted lefty who pitched for the Pirates from 1912 through 1924, finishing up with the Cubs two years later. Four times a 20-game winner, Cooper's lifetime record is 216–178.

Charlie Hollocher, Cub shortstop from 1918 to 1924. Described in glowing terms by his contemporaries, Hollacher's career was aborted by injuries when he was just twenty-eight years old. Lifetime batting average: .304.

Sherry Magee. Magee, an outfielder, joined the Phillies in 1904 and played with them until 1914, when he was traded to the Braves. He finished up with the Reds in 1919. A solid hitter, he led the league with a .331 batting average in 1910. He also led in RBIs three times. Lifetime average: .291.

Jimmy Ring, hard-throwing right-hander who pitched in the National League from 1917 through 1928, working for the Reds, Phillies, Giants, and Cardinals. Jimmy won 18 for a last-place Phillie club in 1923.

Max Carey, champion base-stealer with the Pirates from 1910 through 1926, when he was traded to Brooklyn. Carey, a switch-hitting outfielder, led the league in stolen bases ten times.

Cincinnati left-handers Walter ("Dutch") Ruether (left) and Harry ("Slim") Sallee in 1919. Dutch won 19 that year and Slim 21 as the Reds won the pennant.

Dolf Luque, curve-balling right-hander. Dolf, one of the first native-born Cubans to make it big in the major leagues, pitched from 1914 through 1935 for the Braves, Reds, Dodgers, and Giants. Luque was 27–8 in 1923 for the Reds, for whom he had his best years. Lifetime record: 194–179.

Horace ("Hod") Eller pitched for Cincinnati from 1917 through 1921. He was 20–9 for the 1919 pennant winners.

Jesse Barnes, a solid right-handed pitcher with the Braves, Giants, and Dodgers from 1915 through 1927. Jesse was 25–9 for McGraw in 1919, with a lifetime record of 153–149.

Burleigh Grimes, who pitched for six National League teams from 1916 through 1934. Five times a 20-game winner, Burleigh's lifetime record is 270–212.

Virgil Barnes, Jesse's brother. He pitched for the Giants and Braves from 1919 through 1928, with his best outing a 16–10 mark in 1924.

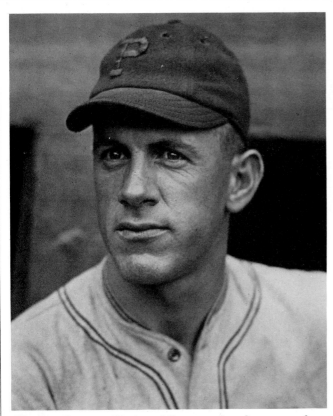

Charlie Grimm, National League first baseman from 1918 through 1936, first with Pittsburgh and then Chicago. A slick fielder, Grimm had a lifetime batting average of .290. He later managed the Cubs and Braves.

Fred ("Cy") Williams, outfielder with the Cubs from 1912 to 1917, then the Phillies until 1930. A premier home run hitter, he led the league four times, with a high of 41 in 1923. His lifetime average is .292.

Hal Carlson, National League right-hander with the Pirates, Phillies, and Cubs from 1917 through 1930. Lifetime record: 114–120. Carlson was 4–2 in 1930, when he died suddenly on May 28 at the age of thirty-six.

Brooklyn's Leon Cadore.

Boston's Joe Oeschger.

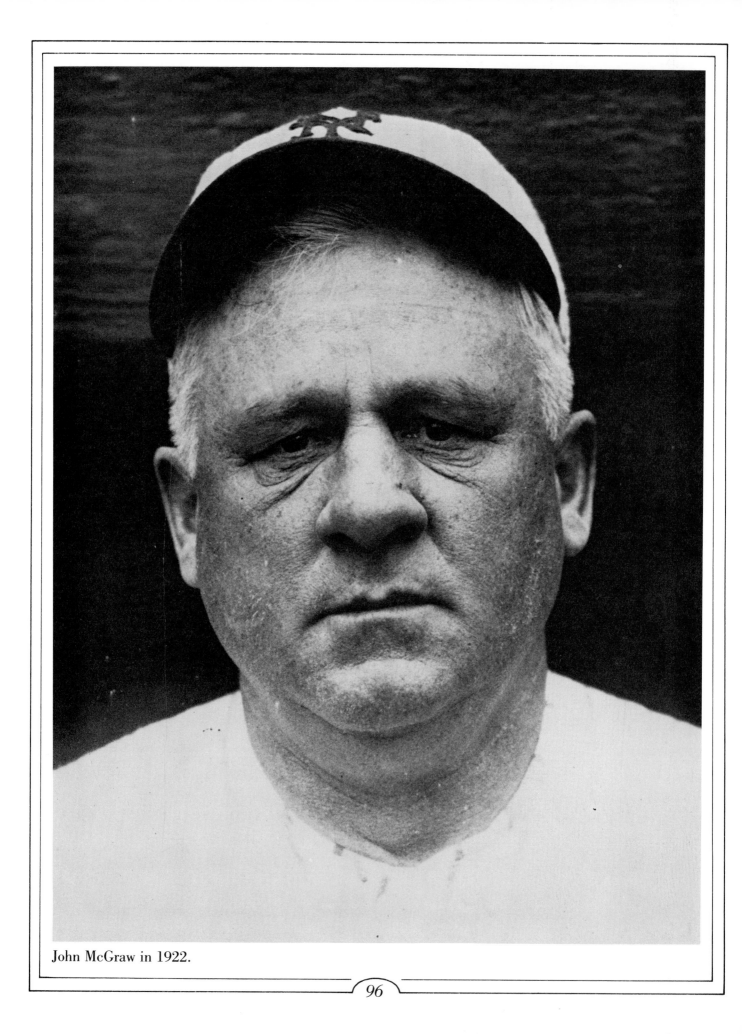

John McGraw in 1922.

4

Thunder at Home Plate

McGraw's Giants became the first club in major-league history to take four consecutive pennants, winning from 1921 through 1924. Although they had some pretty fair pitchers in lefty Art Nehf and right-handers Fred Toney, Jesse Barnes, Rosy Ryan, and Jack Bentley, these Giant teams did it primarily with their bats. McGraw's clubs in the early part of that hard-hitting decade were particularly strong at the plate. Pitching aside (only Nehf in 1921 was a 20-game winner during the four pennant years), they were undoubtedly McGraw's greatest teams. Swinging the heavy timber for John J. was a lineup chockful of future Hall of Famers: George Kelly, Dave Bancroft, Ross Youngs, Hack Wilson, Frank Frisch, Bill Terry, and Travis Jackson, along with Irish Meusel, Frank Snyder, George Burns, and Heinie Groh, who in 1924 was low man in the starting lineup with a .284 average.

Youngs was a nonstop hustler, spiritual forerunner of Pete Rose, and one of McGraw's favorite players. Youngs was so remorseless in his hustle that he earned the nickname "Pep." The stocky Texan's career, however, was cut short by a kidney disease that forced his retirement after the 1926 season; and on October 27, 1927, he died at the age of thirty. Those who entered McGraw's Polo Grounds office in the old man's declining years reported there were but two pictures on the wall: one of Christy Mathewson, the other of Ross Youngs.

Frisch was another diamond fireball, as relentless as Youngs and even more gifted. A switch-hitting infielder with speed to burn, he was considered by his contemporaries the finest National League ballplayer of his era and for many the first pick for any all-star team. The New York-born, Fordham-educated

Dutchman could do it all. Frisch's competitive fire burned at white-hot heat; he had a pride that matched his talent, a reluctance to accept what he felt was unjust criticism, and a tartness of tongue he refused to restrain for anyone, least of all John McGraw. Their clubhouse battles grew until the two were going at each other with sulfurous intensity. It finally came to the point where McGraw and the player he so highly admired and valued could no longer bear to be near each other. When Frisch was finally traded after the 1926 season, he had become so compelling a performer that the man he was traded for was none other than the mighty Rogers Hornsby himself.

By 1926 Hornsby had become the Cardinals' playing manager and in that year drove the team to their first pennant and a stunning World Series victory over the Yankees. What the caustic, brutally frank slugger had been doing to National League pitchers since the beginning of the decade amounted to assault and battery. He had followed up his .370 batting championship in 1920 with scorching figures of .397, .401, .384, .424 (modern baseball's pinnacle figure), and .403. In 1922 his 42 home runs and 152 runs batted in set new league records.

A fanatic when it came to hitting, Hornsby refused to attend the movies because he was afraid it might hurt his eyes, and he limited his reading to the racing form. Baseball was his business. He disdained that traditional delight of many ballplayers, golf, saying, "When I hit a ball I want somebody else to chase it." Without a weakness at the plate, he could not be pitched to, although opposing third basemen suggested it be outside, hoping the Cardinal slugging machine would send his bullet shots in the opposite direction. He was one of a handful of hitters in the game's history—Babe Ruth and Ted Williams were two others—who could stop all the action on a ball field when he stepped into the cage during batting practice. Teammates, opponents,

fans—everybody was fascinated by the sight of "the Rajah" with a bat in his hand.

With the pitchers unable to adapt to the lively ball, earned-run averages swelled along with batting averages as it became a hitter's game, and the fans loved it, attendance shooting up to record heights all around the league. In 1927 the Cubs became the first National League team to draw more than one million paying customers.

In 1922 the league batted a composite .292, led by Pittsburgh's .308 team batting average. McGraw's tenth and final flag in 1924 was attended by an end-of-the-season scandal that for a few days threatened the Giants' World Series appearance. Fighting the Dodgers down to the wire, the Giants were in Philadelphia for the season's final series. In pregame practice New York's Jimmy O'Connell, a twenty-three-year-old reserve outfielder for whose minor-league contract the Giants had shelled out $75,000, told Phillies shortstop Heinie Sand there was $500 in it for Heinie if he did not bear down too hard. Sand reported the bribe attempt to his manager, Art Fletcher; Fletcher took it to the league president and eventually it landed in Landis' lap.

A few days later, with the Giants now having already clinched the pennant, Landis took testimony at the Waldorf-Astoria Hotel in New York. O'Connell, a rather naïve sort, claimed he had been put up to it by coach Cozy Dolan. Dolan pleaded a faulty memory, which enraged Landis. O'Connell also implicated Frisch, Kelly, and Youngs, but the three stars were exonerated. There was some suggestion later that the three, along with some other Giants, might have made some facetious comments to O'Connell about offering a bribe to Sand and that the gullible Jimmy had taken it seriously. In any event, O'Connell and Dolan were barred forever from organized ball. Once more Landis had acted quickly and decisively to reaffirm the game's integrity.

The hard-hitting Pirates finally broke Mc-

Graw's spell and derailed the Giants' bid for a fifth-straight flag in 1925. Compiling a team average of .307, the Pirates coasted in 8½ games ahead of New York. The Pirate lineup was studded with glittering batting averages: first baseman George Grantham's .326, shortstop Glenn Wright's .308, third baseman Pie Traynor's .320, outfielder Kiki Cuyler's .357, outfielder Max Carey's .343, outfielder Clyde Barnhart's .325, catcher Earl Smith's .313. Behind the solid if unspectacular pitching of Lee Meadows, Ray Kremer, Johnny Morrison, Emil Yde, and Vic Aldridge, this powerhouse club muscled their way to the top.

The twenty-five-year-old Traynor was steadily putting together the record at the plate and in the field that would ultimately lead to his being the automatic choice as baseball's all-time third baseman. Quick, agile, and sure-handed around the bag, Traynor teamed with the gifted Wright to give the Pirates a virtually airtight left side.

It was worth a pitcher's life to take the mound in that hit-happy decade. Nevertheless, one National League pitcher stood out among all others—Brooklyn's Clarence ("Dazzy") Vance. This big, high-kicking, fireballing right-hander did not make the big leagues for keeps until 1922, when he was thirty-one years old. Nevertheless, he went on to win 197 games and a niche in the Hall of Fame. Dazzy led in strikeouts his first seven years in the league, having his peak season in 1924, when he was 28–6 and led the pack in wins, earned-run average, complete games, and strikeouts with 262. To give an indication of how much Vance had on the ball that year, only one other pitcher in the league, teammate Burleigh Grimes, struck out over 86 batters that season, Grimes fanning 135.

Rogers Hornsby took over as manager of the Cardinals in midseason 1925 and brought them in fourth. Managing apparently was not too heavy a distraction for Rog, as he won his second Triple Crown (his first came in 1922). A year later he drove the club to their first

pennant, finishing two games up on Cincinnati despite a comparatively poor year for himself (he batted only .317). The Cardinal win meant that now every team in the league had won at least one pennant.

The Cardinal team was beginning to show the influence of its former manager and current general manager, Branch Rickey. Rickey, arguably the finest intellect ever to come into the game, had a few years before begun implementing the idea of a farm system in which to develop his own players. Hitherto, minor-league clubs, most of them independently owned, had sold their major-league prospects to the big teams. It was Rickey's idea for the Cardinals to buy and run their own farm clubs where they would develop their players. The Rickey credo was to sign any youngster who was swift of foot and strong of arm, for these were the God-given talents. Hitting and fielding, he felt, could be taught. In time, the Cardinal farm system would extend to 50 teams at all levels of the minor leagues, with more than 800 players under contract.

One of the mainstays of the Cardinal pitching staff in 1926, however, was not a young man out of the farm system but a thirty-nine-year-old battle-scarred veteran, Grover Cleveland Alexander. Worn, tired, by now an alcoholic and epileptic, Alex had clashed with the Cubs' new manager, Joe McCarthy. Ever the disciplinarian, McCarthy felt compelled to get rid of his veteran. When asked years later whether Alexander observed the rules, Joe chuckled and said, "Sure. He obeyed the rules. But they were always Alex's rules." So Alexander put the cork in his bottle and shifted over to St. Louis, where he won nine games and helped put the Cardinals into the World Series, a series he immortalized with his memorable strikeout of Tony Lazzeri in the seventh game.

A sharp-hitting Pittsburgh team won the pennant in 1927 with a .305 team batting average, led by sophomore outfielder Paul

Waner, who led the league with a .380 average. Playing alongside Paul in the Pirate outfield was his younger brother, Lloyd, a rookie. Young Lloyd broke in with a .355 mark. The slightly built, cat-eyed Waner brothers connected for 460 hits in their first season together. The Cardinals, with Frisch at second now instead of Hornsby, fell just 1½ games short at the finish. The Giants, with Hornsby at second base and batting .361, were two games behind.

McGraw was frustrated by two games again in 1928 in his bid for an eleventh pennant, as the Cardinals, driven by the fiery Frisch, won their second pennant in three years. The Cards had the RBI champ in first baseman Jim Bottomley, who knocked in 136 and tied Chicago's Hack Wilson for the home run lead with 31. The St. Louis farm system had also turned up outfielder Chick Hafey, one of the finest outfielders ever to perform in the National League. A line-drive hitter with a line-drive arm, Chick batted .337.

One year of the outspoken Hornsby had been enough for McGraw, and in January 1928 Rogers was traded to the Braves, his third team in three years. The change of venue made little difference; the thirty-two-year-old slugger took his seventh and last batting championship with a .387 average.

Joe McCarthy's Cubs put on a heavy attack to take the 1929 pennant by 10½ games. Joe's outfield of Kiki Cuyler, Hack Wilson, and Riggs Stephenson batted .360, .345, and .362 respectively. On second base for the Cubs was none other than Rogers Hornsby, acquired from Boston the previous November for five players and $200,000. Rog brought along his .380 bat, hitting exactly that. Topping the league, however, was Philadelphia's Lefty O'Doul, with a sale-price .398 average. The fifth-place Phillies overall batted .309, with O'Doul paced by young Chuck Klein's .356 mark. Hitting records were beginning to fall like autumn leaves now as more and more life was pumped into the ball, despite official protestations that nothing had been changed. Klein's 43 home runs were a new league high, as were O'Doul's 254 hits. The league hit 754 home runs, an increase of 144 over the previous season.

What happened in 1930, however, made 1929 look like a time of popguns. Baseballs left National League parks as though there were launching pads at home plate. The league as a whole batted .303 as six teams, led by New York's .319 team batting average, hit over .300. The previous year's home run total of 754 was wiped out by a new figure of 892 circuit shots, a mark that stood until 1949. A batting average of .330 or .340 was almost a sign of infirmity. The leading batters in 1930 were Bill Terry, .401; Babe Herman, .393; Chuck Klein, .386; Lefty O'Doul, .383; Fred Lindstrom, .379. Fifteen men batted over .340, 17 drove in over 100 runs. The league ERA averaged out to almost five runs per game.

King of the hill in this bat-happy, shell-shocked season was Chicago's 5'6" fireplug center fielder, Lewis ("Hack") Wilson. Hack had enjoyed some fine seasons, but in 1930 he went clear out of sight. Hack hit 56 home runs; it was the fifth time in 19 years that a new league record in roundtrippers had been set, and this one was destined to stand. Wilson's appetite for driving in runs was positively insatiable; he set a major-league standard of 190 RBIs, a record that has not been even remotely threatened since Hank Greenberg's 183 total in 1937.

While none of his National League opponents enjoyed Wilson's monumental season, John McGraw no doubt took it hardest. Hack came up with the Giants in 1923, showed some promise, and after a few years was farmed out for more seasoning. McGraw had every intention of bringing Hack back, but a clerical error by the Giants' front office left him exposed to the draft and the Cubs grabbed him at bargain-basement rates in October 1925. What McGraw said when this happened has not been recorded, but it must have been inspiring.

Dazzy Vance, Brooklyn's thirty-nine-year-old hardballer, had the best earned-run average that year, a remarkable 2.61 mark, followed by New York's screwballing lefty Carl Hubbell, on the brink of greatness now, who logged a second-best 3.76.

The Cardinals, with eight .300 hitters in the lineup and four more on the bench getting a game when they could, edged past the Cubs by a mere two games to win the pennant. St. Louis' pennant clinching enabled them to start a nineteen-year-old right-hander in the last game of the season. His name was Jerome Dean, he was known as "Dizzy," and his debut was a telltale one. The youngster went nine, allowed one run and three hits, and won his game.

In spite of fan enthusiasm over the batting barrage—the league drew 5.5 million customers, 500,000 more than the year before—the baseball establishment became appalled by the whistle of line drives and over the winter decided to squeeze a little of the juice from the ball.

George Kelly, first baseman on McGraw's 1921–1924 pennant winners. George played from 1916 through 1932 with five teams. His 23 home runs led in 1921. He hit over .300 seven times, with a lifetime average of .297.

Frank Frisch, 19 National League years with the Giants and Cardinals, 13 years over .300, with a lifetime average of .316.

Ross Youngs, McGraw's rugged, hustling outfield favorite from 1917 through 1926. He batted over .300 in eight of his nine full seasons, with a high of .356 in 1924 and a lifetime mark of .322.

Emil ("Irish") Meusel, hard-hitting outfielder with the Phillies, Giants, and Dodgers from 1918 to 1927. Irish hit over .300 six times and finished with a .310 lifetime.

Irish Meusel scoring in the fifth game of the 1922 World Series against the Yankees. The catcher is Wally Schang. Frank Frisch is standing behind the umpire, while third base coach Hughie Jennings is running up to have a better look.

Earl Smith, who caught for four National League teams from 1919 through 1930. His lifetime average is .303.

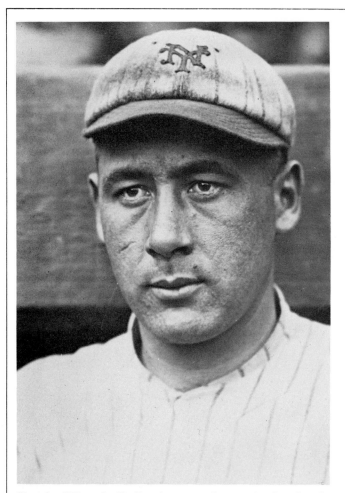

Frank ("Pancho") Snyder, catcher with the Cardinals and Giants from 1912 through 1927.

Right-hander Pete Donohue, a three-time 20-game winner for the Reds in the 1920s. He pitched from 1921 through 1932, with a lifetime record of 134–118.

Action at third base in this 1922 game between the Dodgers and Giants. Brooklyn's Otto Miller is just beating Frank Frisch's diving tag.

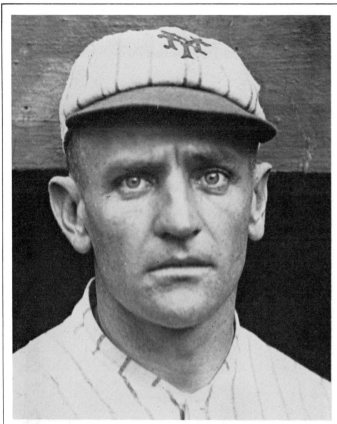

Giant outfielder Casey Stengel in 1922.

Johnny Morrison. They called this Pittsburgh right-hander "Jughandle Johnny" for the big curve he threw. He threw it well enough in 1923 to win 25 games. Johnny pitched from 1920 to 1930, mostly with the Pirates.

Alvin ("Cozy") Dolan. Dolan had a modest career with several clubs between 1909 and 1915, then was booted out of baseball as a Giant coach in 1924 for participation in a bribe offer.

Jimmy O'Connell, the talented young Giant outfielder barred from baseball for allegedly offering a bribe in 1924.

Rogers Hornsby.

Dazzy Vance.

Judge Kenesaw Mountain Landis.

Left-hander Jack Bentley; he pitched briefly but effectively for the Giants from 1923 to 1925.

Wilfred ("Rosy") Ryan, a right-hander with the Giants from 1919 to 1924. Rosy led in ERA in 1922 with 3.01.

George Kelly scoring in the 1924 World Series against Washington. The man biting the dust is catcher Muddy Ruel.

Jack Scott, who pitched for five National League teams between 1916 and 1929. In 1923 his 16–7 record helped the Giants to the pennant. Lifetime he was 103–109.

Right-hander Hugh McQuillan pitched for the Braves and Giants from 1918 through 1927. He helped the Giants to pennants in 1922, 1923, and 1924.

Cliff Heathcote. An outfielder, Cliff played with the Cardinals, Cubs, Reds, and Phillies from 1918 through 1932.

Travis Jackson, stellar shortstop with the Giants from 1922 to 1936. He hit over .300 six times.

Hughie Critz, second baseman with Cincinnati from 1924 to 1930, then with the Giants until 1935.

Frank ("Jakie") May, a lefty who pitched for the Cardinals, Reds, and Cubs from 1917 to 1932.

John ("Sheriff") Blake, Chicago Cub right-hander of the 1920s.

Infielder George Grantham. George came up with the Cubs in 1923, joined the Pirates in 1925, and later played for the Reds and Giants, retiring in 1934. He had eight consecutive years over .300 and a lifetime of .302.

Submarine-ball pitcher Carl Mays joined the Reds in 1924 after nine years in the American League and promptly won 20. He finished up with the Giants in 1929.

Hack Wilson with the Giants in 1925.

Lee Meadows, who pitched for the Cardinals, Phillies, and Pirates from 1915 to 1929. His best was a 20–9 year for the Pirates in 1926. Lifetime record: 188–180.

Hazen ("Kiki") Cuyler, one of the finest all-around ballplayers in the National League from 1921 to 1938. He came up with the Pirates and was traded to the Cubs in 1928. Later he played for the Reds and Dodgers. Four times he led in stolen bases and four times he batted over .350. Lifetime average: .321.

Remy ("Ray") Kremer, Pittsburgh right-hander from 1924 to 1933. He was 20–6 in 1926 and 20–12 in 1930. Lifetime he stands at 143–85.

The cream of third basemen, Pittsburgh's Harold ("Pie") Traynor. Pie spent his full career with the Pirates, from 1920 to 1937, batting over .300 ten times, with a high of .366 in 1930. His lifetime average is .320.

Glenn Wright, hard-hitting, strong-armed shortstop with Pittsburgh and Brooklyn from 1924 to 1933. Lifetime average: .294.

Two managers posing together on Opening Day 1925: Art Fletcher (left) of the Phillies and Dave Bancroft of the Braves. Dave was a top-flight shortstop from 1915 to 1930, starring with the Phillies, Giants, Braves, and Dodgers.

Fred Lindstrom. He joined the Giants in 1924 at the age of eighteen and went on to stardom as a third baseman and outfielder, later playing with the Pirates, Cubs, and Dodgers. In 1930 he batted .379 and for the second time collected 231 hits. Lifetime batting average: .311.

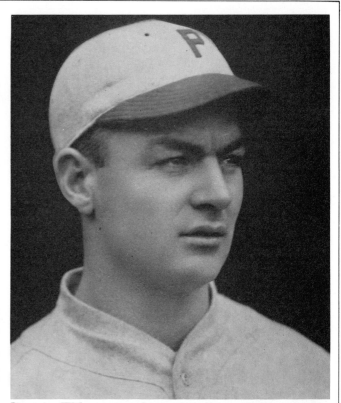

Jimmie Wilson, crack catcher from 1923 to 1940 with the Phillies, Cardinals, and Reds.

"Sunny Jim" Bottomley, hard-hitting first baseman with the Cardinals from 1922 to 1932, then with the Reds until 1935. He hit over .300 nine times, with a high of .371 in 1923. He drove in over 100 runs six straight times and batted .310 lifetime.

Billy Southworth. Billy roamed the outfield for the Pirates, Braves, Giants, and Cardinals from 1918 to 1929, batting over .300 six times. Later he managed the Cardinals and Braves, winning four pennants.

Billy Southworth touching home plate after clouting a home run in the second game of the 1926 World Series against the Yankees. Patting him on the shoulder is Rogers Hornsby.

Bob O'Farrell, for 21 years a catcher in the National League. Bob came up with the Cubs in 1915 and later played for the Cardinals, Giants, and Reds.

Wee Willie Sherdel, St. Louis Cardinal lefty from 1918 to 1930. Willie's best year was 1928, when he was 21–10. Lifetime he was 165–146.

Slick-fielding, steady-hitting Taylor Douthit played the outfield for the Cardinals from 1923 to 1931, finishing up with the Reds and Cubs in 1933. His lifetime average is .291.

Grover Cleveland Alexander in 1926.

A fine spring day and a full house at the Polo Grounds as the Giants play the Braves in April 1926.

Jesse ("Pop") Haines pitched for the Cardinals from 1920 to 1937, winning 20 three times. Lifetime record: 210–158.

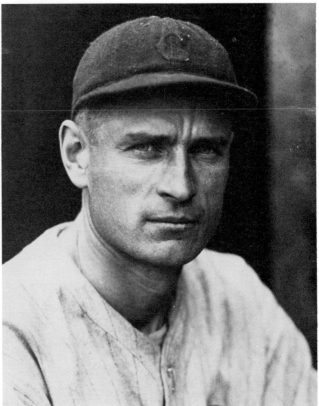

Wally Pipp, the man who lost his Yankee first base job to Lou Gehrig. Wally played for the Reds from 1926 to 1928.

Chuck Dressen, Cincinnati's regular third baseman in the late 1920s. He later managed the Reds and Dodgers, among others.

Long-time American League ace "Bullet" Joe Bush. He pitched for the Pirates and Giants in 1926 and 1927.

Veteran American League first baseman Stuffy McInnis. He played for the Braves, Pirates, and Phillies from 1923 to 1927.

Eugene ("Bubbles") Hargrave, a .300-hitting catcher with Cincinnati in the 1920s. In 1926 Bubbles' .353 batting average made him the first catcher ever to win a batting title. His lifetime average is .310.

Lloyd and Paul Waner.

John Heydler, National League president from 1918 to 1934.

Fred Fitzsimmons, a knuckle-balling right-hander who pitched for the Giants from 1925 to 1937, when he was traded to the Dodgers, for whom he pitched until 1943. Fred was 217–146 lifetime.

Former American Leaguer Joe Harris played first base for the 1927 pennant-winning Pirates and batted .326.

Right-hander Larry Benton, a 25-game winner for the Giants in 1928. Larry also pitched for the Braves and Reds in a career that ran from 1923 to 1935. Lifetime record: 127–128.

Francis ("Lefty") O'Doul, one of the smoothest of hitters. Lefty was in the National League with the Giants, Phillies, and Dodgers from 1928 through 1934. He led with .398 in 1929 and .368 in 1932. He also batted .383 in 1930 and had a lifetime average of .349.

Riggs Stephenson, Chicago Cub outfielder from 1926 to 1934 and a .300 hitter every year except the last. Riggs batted .362 in 1929 and .367 in 1930.

Guy Bush, Chicago Cub right-hander from 1923 to 1934, and later for four other teams. Winning steadily, Bush peaked with a 20–12 record in 1933. His lifetime record is 176–136.

George Sisler (left) and Rogers Hornsby when both were with the Braves in 1928.

Right-hander Charlie Root pitched for the Cubs from 1926 to 1941. He won 26 in 1927 and was 201–160 lifetime.

Adam Comorosky, outfielder with Pittsburgh and Cincinnati from 1926 to 1935. He led with 23 triples in 1930.

Pat Malone, Cub righty from 1928 to 1934. In 1929–1930 Pat was 22–10 and 20–9, leading in victories each season.

James Francis ("Shanty") Hogan, catcher for the Braves and Giants from 1925 to 1935. Shanty batted .339 in 1930 and was .295 lifetime.

Phil Collins, called "Fidgety Phil." A right-hander, he was one of the mainstays of the Phillies' staff from 1929 to 1935.

Don Hurst, Phillie first baseman from 1928 to 1934. Don batted .339 in 1932 and led the league with 143 runs batted in.

Earl ("Sparky") Adams, infielder with the Cubs, Pirates, Cardinals, and Reds from 1922 to 1934. He batted .286 lifetime.

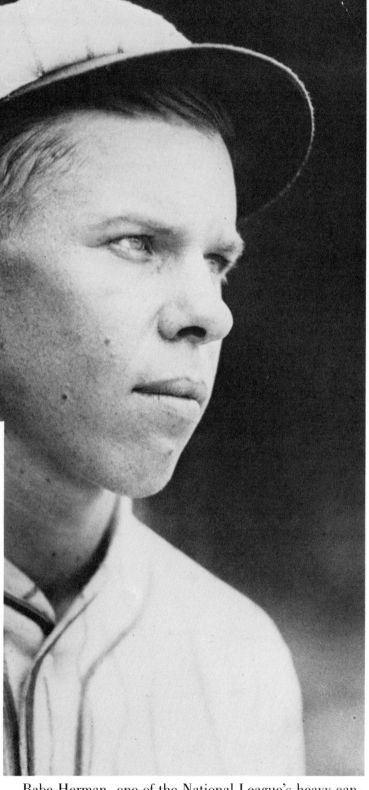

Charles ("Chick") Hafey, one of the great National League outfielders of all time. He played with the Cardinals from 1924 to 1931 and then with the Reds from 1932 to 1937. He hit over .300 nine times, led the league in 1931 with a .349 average, and had a lifetime mark of .317.

Babe Herman, one of the National League's heavy cannoneers from 1926 to 1936 with Brooklyn, Cincinnati, Chicago, and Pittsburgh. Babe did his best work for the Dodgers in 1929 and 1930, when he batted .381 and .393. He batted over .300 eight times and has a lifetime average of .324.

After four years with Detroit, righty Sylvester Johnson came to the National League with the Cardinals in 1926, later pitching for the Reds and Phillies until 1940.

Al Lopez, superb catcher for Brooklyn, Boston, and Pittsburgh from 1928 to 1946. Al caught 1,861 games in the National League, a league record.

Wally Berger, a long-balling outfielder who had his best years with the Braves from 1930 to 1937. His 38 homers in 1930 set a record for rookies and his 34 in 1935 led the league. His batting average for 11 years is an even .300.

Chuck Klein, Philadelphia's mighty slugger. Chuck played from 1928 to 1944 with the Phillies, Cubs, and Pirates. He had his greatest years with the Phillies from 1928 through 1933. He batted .386 in 1930 and led the league with .368 in 1933. He collected 200 or more hits his first five full years in the league, leading in home runs four of those years. Lifetime average: .320.

Pepper Martin. Thirteen years a Cardinal, six times a .300 hitter.

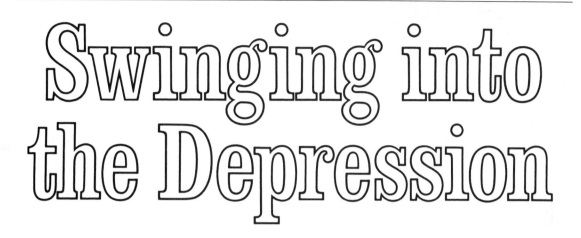

5

Swinging into the Depression

Batting averages dropped in 1931, and so did attendance, and so did the nation's financial health. The nation began sinking deeper and deeper into a bleak and deadening depression. If it was a time when America needed a common, salt-of-the-earth man for a hero, it found him in baseball. A fresh-minted graduate of the Cardinal farm system named John Leonard ("Pepper") Martin broke into the St. Louis outfield, batted .300, helped them to a pennant, and then ran and batted like a fury in the World Series. For seven days in October the Oklahoma farmboy captured the national imagination with a performance of dynamic, uninhibited splendor, whacking Connie Mack's Philadelphia Athletics for 12 hits and stealing five bases.

Martin was a perfect addition to a Cardinal team gearing up to "Gashouse Gang" notoriety. Frisch continued to be the driving force at second base, while Hafey won the closest batting race in history, his .3489 average just topping Bill Terry's .3486 and teammate Jim Bottomley's .3482.

A semblance of order had been restored to batting averages, the league dropping 26 points to a composite mark of .277. The Cubs were tops with .289, with the stumpy Wilson taking the most precipitous fall from the heights, ending with barely noticeable numbers in home runs (13) and runs batted in (61). Hack batted in 129 fewer men than he did in 1930, though he still scored high in the booze league, a predilection that severely hindered his career.

The year saw the retirement of Wilbert Robinson as manager of the Dodgers, ending a tenure that had begun in 1914. A year later, on June 3, 1932, another managerial career—the most colorful and controversial in all of baseball—came to an end.

John McGraw was 59 years old. He was tired, worn out, physically ailing. And the times had changed. The day of the tyrannical, uncompromisingly authoritarian manager was passing. Players no longer submitted passively to brutal tongue-lashings. McGraw had been unable to contend with Frisch. Fred Lindstrom, the Giants' brilliant third baseman, refused to sit silently while his skipper humiliated him. Most rebellious of all was first baseman Bill Terry, the greatest of McGraw's ballplayers. The proud, intelligent, independent Terry would not take McGraw's fulminations. For several years the two barely spoke to each other.

So it was a stunning surprise when the departing McGraw, given the privilege of choosing his successor, named Terry. Ever the uncompromising baseball man, John J. buried personal differences and selected the man he felt best suited for the job.

It was a year of unexpected managerial moves. With the Cubs in first place on August 2, Manager Rogers Hornsby, who had replaced Joe McCarthy, was canned after a series of policy disputes with club president William Veeck (father of Bill Veeck, whose promotional genius shook up the baseball establishment in the postwar years). Hornsby's replacement, first baseman Charlie Grimm, continued the good work and guided the club to the pennant, finishing four games ahead of Pittsburgh.

It was a good year for rookies in the National League. Chicago had twenty-two-year-old Billy Herman at second; Pittsburgh brought up a twenty-year-old shortstop named Arky Vaughan, after Wagner, probably the league's greatest shortstop; Brooklyn had a twenty-one-year-old smoke thrower named Van Lingle Mungo; and St. Louis unveiled for keeps the twenty-one-year-old Dizzy Dean.

Dean, son of an Arkansas sharecropper, was as colorful and endearing a character as ever played in the big leagues. Possessed of phenomenal natural ability, with a canny

sixth sense on the mound to go along with his hopping fast ball and snapping curve, he soon became, with the fading of Babe Ruth, the game's greatest draw, his wide-open homespun personality one of the few pure joys to be found in a depression-stricken America. Dean, who sometimes predicted his shutouts in advance ("It ain't braggin' if you go out and do it after sayin' it," he insisted), was 18–15 in his maiden voyage, leading in innings pitched, strikeouts, and shutouts, while laboring for a sixth-place club.

A year later McGraw's judgment was borne out. Rising from a sixth-place tie with the Cardinals in 1932, Terry led his Giants to the 1933 pennant, five games ahead of a Pittsburgh team that was still blasting away but was forever shy of front-rank pitching. The Pirates outhit the Giants by .285 to .263, but the difference was New York's pitching. Carl Hubbell screwballed his way to a 23–12 record, while right-hander Hal Schumacher won 19 and knuckle baller Fred Fitzsimmons won 16.

The quiet, self-effacing Hubbell, personally and stylistically the exact antithesis of his chief rival, Dean, hurled ten shutouts and led with a fine 1.66 earned-run average, the league's best since Alexander's 1.22 in 1915. On July 2 at the Polo Grounds, Hubbell pitched his greatest game, shutting out the Cardinals 1–0 in 18 innings. Tex Carleton pitched the first 16 for St. Louis before giving way to Jesse Haines, the losing pitcher. In weaving his 18-inning masterpiece Hubbell walked none and surrendered but six hits.

The league's top hitter in 1933 was Philadelphia's Chuck Klein, a Triple Crown winner with a .368 batting average, 28 home runs, and 120 runs batted in. The Phillies rewarded their star slugger by selling him to the Cubs after the season. This was a pattern with the dollar-poor Phillies through most of the decade—develop a star player and then peddle him for needed cash.

With Frank Frisch managing and with

Branch Rickey's farm system pouring in the talent, the Cardinals soared to the top in 1934, winning their fifth pennant in nine years. This was the Gashouse Gang of lore and legend now, a team of vivid, raucous characters headed by Frisch's bristling spirit and buoyed by Dizzy Dean's scintillating 30–7 season. From the farm system had come Dizzy's younger brother Paul, quiet and soft-spoken but nicknamed "Daffy" all the same, and a 19-game winner with a swifty they said was quicker than his big brother's. And there was Joe Medwick, a muscular left fielder with a prickly personality and a smoldering bat that made him the National League's premier buster of the 1930s. In 1934 Joe warmed up for greatness with a .319 year and 106 runs batted in. At shortstop the Cardinals had Leo Durocher, slick-fielding, light-hitting, and heavy-mouthed. Blithe spirits like first baseman Ripper Collins and Pepper Martin helped give this low-paid Depression club a flair and personality few baseball teams have ever achieved.

The Cardinals won it by two games over Terry's Giants, and it was the last two days of the season that made it all worthwhile for a Brooklyn Dodger team struggling in sixth place. In the spring, Terry had let slip a wisecrack about his crosstown rivals. When asked a question about the Dodgers, the normally dour Giant skipper said "Is Brooklyn still in the league?"

Truly in the proletarian spirit of the day, the lowly Dodgers under Casey Stengel stung the lordly Giants on the season's final weekend. The Giants and Cardinals were in a flat-footed tie for first place, with the Cardinals playing their last two games against the Reds and the Giants opposing the Dodgers. Throngs of leather-lunged Dodger fans filled the Polo Grounds to cheer their heroes and taunt Terry and the Giants, reminding Memphis Bill that they were still very much in the league. In two memorable and, for Brooklyn fans, soul-satisfying games, the Bums twice topped the Giants while the Cardinals were winning it all against Cincinnati.

"I would have come in to console you," Stengel later said to Terry, "but I thought better of it."

"Just as well," Terry said. "If you had, you would have been thrown out on your ass."

The year that ended so disappointingly for the Giants had begun on a sad note. On February 25 John McGraw died of uremia at his New Rochelle, New York, home, two months before his sixty-first birthday.

In 1935 the old magician came to the National League. He was fat, forty, slow, and his reflexes were shot. But there was one last blast of thunder and swirl of smoke before he disappeared forever. He was Babe Ruth, released by the Yankees the year before and signed by the Boston Braves with the hope he would put some spin in the turnstiles. But it was all gone for Ruth. He bumbled through 28 games and a .181 batting average before calling it quits early in June. Before that, however, there was his last eruption at Forbes Field on May 25, when he sent soaring three mammoth home runs. Ruth's last team, ironically, proved to be the league's most inept ever—the 1935 Boston Braves lost 115 games, the record for the 154-game schedule. Eight years before, the Babe had starred on the greatest of all teams, the 1927 New York Yankees.

At the other end of the spectrum in 1935 were the Cubs, who tore off a 21-game September winning streak that carried them past the Cardinals and the Giants, who had been fighting it out all year. Chicago second baseman Billy Herman batted .341 and righties Bill Lee and Lon Warneke were 20-game winners. Dizzy Dean "slumped" to a 28–12 record while vainly trying to hurl the Cardinals to the pennant, and Joe Medwick hit full stride with a .353 batting average. Joe, however, was a distant second to Pittsburgh's Arky Vaughan, who took the batting crown with a very elite .385 mark, highest ever for a National League shortstop and an average that, through the 1982 season, remained unmatched in the league.

The big news in baseball in 1935 came out of Cincinnati, where the Reds' general manager, Larry MacPhail, a brash, noisy, brilliant innovator and visionary, had cajoled and browbeat the conservative baseball establishment into accepting a quaint idea called night ball. Although night baseball had already proved itself successful in the minor leagues, the major-league owners were skeptical. They finally relented to the point where they permitted their clubs to each play one game under Cincinnati's lights—almost as if they were humoring MacPhail. On May 24, with President Roosevelt himself pushing a button in the White House that activated the lamps at Crosley Field, the era of night ball began. The skeptics called it a novelty and a fad that would pass. Within 13 years every big-league club except the Cubs had installed lights in their parks.

Led by Carl Hubbell (aptly nicknamed "the Meal Ticket"), the Giants won pennants in 1936 and 1937. At the very summit of his career in 1936, Hubbell was 26–6, closing out the season with a 16-game winning streak. He won his first eight in 1937, running his two-year win streak to 24, on his way to a 22–8 record. Terry's teams were powered during these years by Mel Ott, a quiet, likable outfielder with an unorthodox high leg kick and an ability to pull his shots down the Polo Grounds' short right-field line. Only a moderate home run hitter elsewhere, Mel was always a threat at home. He topped the league in the pennant years with 33 and 31 home runs.

Hubbell was joined in the 20-win circle in 1937 by teammate Cliff Melton, a rookie left-hander. It was a memorable year for rookie pitchers, as two Boston Braves newcomers, righties Lou Fette and Jim Turner, each won 20 for the fifth-place Braves. (After that, none of the three ever won more than 14 games a season.)

It was also a tragic year for the league's dominant pitcher, personality, and drawing card. Pitching in the All-Star Game that July, Dizzy Dean was hit on the foot by a low, whistling liner off the bat of Cleveland's Earl Averill. Dean suffered a broken toe. Never overly burdened with common sense, the mighty righty came back too soon, favored the injured foot, and in so doing strained his arm. For all intents and purposes his career was over. He ended the season with a 13–10 record. The following spring the Cardinals unloaded him on the Cubs for nearly $200,000 and several players, including right-hander Curt Davis, a steady winner. When it came to making deals, Branch Rickey had no peer.

Joe Medwick put together his greatest year in 1937, a Triple Crown season that saw him bat .374, hit 31 home runs, and drive in 154 runs. Joe also led with 56 doubles, an impressive total but eight less than the 64 he hit the year before, when he set a National League record that still stands. Teaming with Joe on the Cardinals was another product of the farm system, first baseman Johnny Mize. Big John, one of the most fearsome sluggers of all time (his lifetime slugging average is second only to Hornsby's in National League history), batted .364, hit 25 homers, and drove in 113 runs. Fine numbers all, but overshadowed by Medwick that year.

Through the days of the Depression and the gathering of war clouds over Europe, the game of baseball continued on, following the serene pace of summer. It seemed immune to all of the changes, vibrations, and concussions of the simmering world around it, like some grain of naïveté that was both inviolate and invulnerable. It continued on, following much the same pattern and set of rules that had been laid down (or ordained, so piously were they adhered to) in what seemed in retrospect the untimed days of the nineteenth century. Game after game the ritual was performed, always with that same sense of anticipation just before the delivery of the first pitch.

It would have seemed that by 1938 everything that could possibly happen on a ball field had happened, after tens of thousands of games. But in 1938 the game once again proved it could deliver beribboned thrills and pulsing excitement, the unexpected, the unprecedented. It was in 1938 that a twenty-three-year-old Cincinnati left-hander named Johnny Vander Meer engraved his name on baseball forever. Possessed of blinding speed, Vander Meer's career had been slightly checkered because of wildness. He joined the Cincinnati club in 1937 and came under the guidance of a canny veteran manager, Bill McKechnie, a skilled and patient handler of pitchers.

On June 11 Vander Meer hurled a no-hitter against the Braves, winning by a 3–0 score. A solid achievement, but hardly without precedent, since there had been 20 no-hitters pitched in the league since 1901. Four days later, however, the young lefty baked another cake for himself and applied icing that has remained fresh ever since.

It was, to begin with, a special occasion at Ebbets Field in Brooklyn. Larry MacPhail, by now running the Dodgers, had brought his arc-light revolution to New York and on June 15 the lights went on for the first time. A packed house filled Ebbets Field and the promotional-minded MacPhail celebrated with all kinds of pregame festivities, from bands and speeches to track-and-field events. Then Vander Meer took over and made it a night to remember by writing a page of baseball's most glittering history by hurling his second consecutive no-hitter. Bedeviled by a streak of ninth-inning wildness during which he walked the bases loaded, the young man nevertheless continued firing away and strode off the mound with a 6–0 victory and another no-hitter.

In his next start, against the Braves in Boston, Johnny opened with two more hitless innings. It was after the second inning that

Braves Manager Casey Stengel, passing Vander Meer on the field between innings, said, "We're not trying to beat you, John. We're just trying to get a hit." The hit came in the third, a single by Debs Garms, finally breaking Vandy's spell at 21⅓ hitless innings.

The year also produced a classic case of "pennant theft" by the Chicago Cubs. The victims were the Pittsburgh Pirates, leading the Cubs by a game and a half when the two clubs convened for a three-game series at Wrigley Field on September 27. Starting his first game in over a month, Chicago's sore-armed Dizzy Dean guiled his way to a 2–1 victory. The following day the teams were tied 5–5 in the bottom of the ninth. With two out and darkness approaching, it seemed the game would have to be replayed as part of a doubleheader the next day, a disadvantage for the Cubs, whose pitching staff was worn out. The batter was veteran catcher Gabby Hartnett, also the manager, having taken over the club from Charlie Grimm in midseason. Pirate relief ace Mace Brown whipped across two strikes on Gabby. Brown tried for a third strike, made it a mite too good, and Hartnett, barely able to see the ball in the fading light, swung hard and connected solidly. The ball sailed into the left-field bleachers: the famous "homer in the gloamin'." The Cubs trounced the dispirited Pirates the next day and went on to take the pennant, continuing an odd three-year victory pattern that saw them on top in 1929, 1932, 1935, and 1938.

It was the Cincinnati Reds in 1939 and again in 1940, primarily on the pitching of two remarkable right-handers, Bucky Walters and Paul Derringer, and the steady hitting of first baseman Frank McCormick and catcher Ernie Lombardi.

Walters, who had come to the big leagues as an infielder and failed to make much of an impact with his bat, always impressed his managers with his strong right arm. His pegs across the infield had so much on them that his first basemen sometimes had trouble handling them. Converted to pitching in 1935, when he was with the Phillies (a wise old catcher, Jimmie Wilson, was the manager who talked him into it), Bucky grudgingly went along with what he thought was a bad idea. But he pitched well for his team—they were known as "the Phutile Phillies" in those years—and in June 1938 was dealt to the Reds. A year later he was 27–11, while Derringer was 27–7. In 1940 they fired away to pitch the Reds to another pennant, Bucky winning 22 and Paul 20.

McCormick, a slick-fielding first baseman with a bat as consistent as a ticking clock, broke in as a regular in 1938 and batted .327, .332, and .309, leading the league in hits in each of his first three years. Lombardi, the big, good-natured, slow-moving catcher, was probably the most feared hitter in the league. Ernie hit ferocious line drives, forcing the left side of the infield to play him back on the grass, which was both prudent and tactically sound because of Ernie's painfully slow running speed. In 1938 he became only the second catcher in big-league history to win a batting title with a .342 average. (Cincinnati's Bubbles Hargrave had led in 1926.)

Larry MacPhail's arc-light revolution was catching on. Shedding their traditional conservatism to the tune of spinning turnstiles, the Giants, Pirates, and Cardinals introduced night ball to their fans, joining the Reds, Dodgers, and Phillies as purveyors of after-dark entertainment. They would soon be joined by the Braves, leaving only the Cubs as proponents of daylight ball.

Cub shortstop Billy Jurges being interviewed by announcer Bob Elson in the early 1930s. Jurges played for the Cubs and Giants from 1931 to 1947.

A winning pitcher with losing Braves teams from 1928 to 1935, Ed Brandt had a lifetime record of 121–146. He also pitched for Brooklyn and Pittsburgh.

Billy Herman, one of the great second basemen in National League history. He was with the Cubs from 1931 to 1941, and then with Brooklyn, Boston, and Pittsburgh, retiring as an active player in 1947. Lifetime average: .304.

Stan Hack, a model of consistency for the Cubs at third base from 1932 to 1947, batting .280 or better for 14 consecutive seasons. He batted .301 lifetime.

Floyd ("Arky") Vaughan. The National League's premier shortstop with Pittsburgh from 1932 to 1941, Vaughan batted over .300 in every one of those years, with a league-leading .385 in 1935 his best. He later played for the Dodgers, retiring in 1948 with a .318 lifetime average.

Lon Warneke, a first-class right-hander for the Cubs and Cardinals from 1930 to 1945, twice winning 20 for the Cubs. Lifetime record: 193–121.

Gus Suhr, first baseman with the Pirates and Phillies from 1930 to 1940. At one point Gus appeared in 822 consecutive games for the Pirates, the fourth best iron-man streak in National League history.

James ("Ripper") Collins, colorful first baseman with the Cardinals, Cubs, and Pirates from 1931 to 1941. Rip's big year with the Gashouse Gang was 1934, when he hit .333 and led the league with 35 home runs.

Tony Cuccinello, second baseman with the Reds, Dodgers, Braves, and Giants from 1930 to 1943.

James ("Tex") Carleton, right-hander with the Cardinals, Cubs, and Dodgers from 1932 to 1940. Tex was 100–76 lifetime.

Paul ("Daffy") Dean.

Dizzy Dean.

LeRoy Parmelee, hard-throwing right-hander with the Giants, Cardinals, and Cubs from 1929 to 1937.

Leo Durocher, Cardinal shortstop, in 1934.

Changing of the guard: Bill Terry (left) and John McGraw, soon after Terry took over as Giants manager.

Carl Hubbell. Lifetime record: 253–154.

Frank Demaree, outfielder with four National League teams from 1932 to 1943. Frank batted .350 for the Cubs in 1936.

Left to right: Philadelphia's Dick Bartell, St. Louis' Frank Frisch and Pepper Martin in the uniforms the National League wore for the first All-Star Game in 1933. Bartell was a crackerjack shortstop for the Pirates, Phillies, Giants, and Cubs.

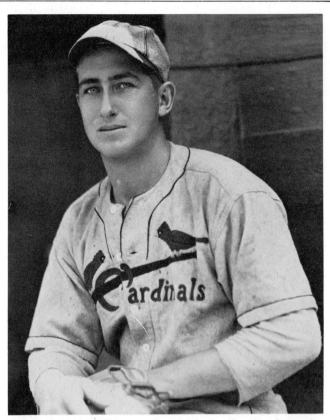

Bill DeLancey, fine catcher with the Cardinals in the middle 1930s whose career was cut short by illness.

Charles ("Red") Lucas, right-hander with the Giants, Braves, Reds, and Pirates from 1923 to 1938. He won 19 for the Reds in 1929. Red was one of the game's great hitting pitchers, frequently used as a pinch hitter, in which capacity he led the league in hits four times. His lifetime batting average is .281, while on the mound he was 157–135.

Bill Walker, southpaw with the Giants and Cardinals from 1927 to 1936. Bill led in ERA in 1929 and 1931.

Durable and popular Phil Cavarretta played first base and outfield for the Cubs from 1934 to 1953. His .355 led the league in 1945. Lifetime average: .293.

Virgil ("Spud") Davis, one of the National League's better hitting catchers. Spud played with the Cardinals, Phillies, Reds, and Pirates from 1928 to 1945, hitting over .300 nine times, with a .349 high in 1933. His lifetime is .308.

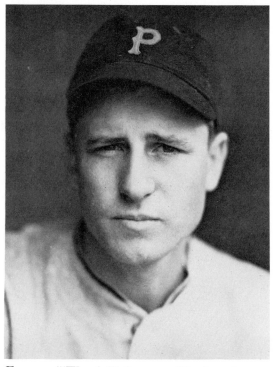

Augie Galan starred with the Cubs from 1934 to 1941, then with Brooklyn through 1946. He later played for the Reds and Giants. Lifetime batting average: .287.

Forrest ("Woody") Jensen, Pittsburgh outfielder from 1931 to 1939. Lifetime average: .285.

A crafty left-hander, Larry French pitched for Pittsburgh from 1929 to 1934, Chicago 1935 to 1941, when he was traded to Brooklyn, where he finished up in 1942. Steady as a rock, his lifetime record is 197–171.

Ford C. Frick, National League president from 1934 to 1951. He served as commissioner from 1951 to 1965.

Dizzy Dean (left) and Frankie Frisch spiffed up for the winter banquet circuit in 1934.

Joe Medwick. Slugger with the Cardinals, Dodgers, Giants, and Braves from 1932 through 1948. Fourteen times a .300 hitter, Joe's lifetime is .324.

Babe Ruth with the Boston Braves in 1935. Babe played 28 games, batted .181, and hit six home runs before retiring in early June.

Five good arms on National League's 1936 All-Star Game pitching staff. Left to right: Van Lingle Mungo, Dizzy Dean, Lon Warneke, Carl Hubbell, and Curt Davis.

Bill Terry watching his "Meal Ticket," Carl Hubbell, loosen up in spring training in 1936.

Three New York Giants killing a rainy day in their hotel room in 1936. Left to right: pitcher Clyde Castleman, shortstop Mark Koenig, catcher Harry Danning.

Jo-Jo Moore, sharp-hitting Giant outfielder from 1930 to 1941. His lifetime average is .298.

Four members of the 1936 pennant-winning New York Giants. Left to right: outfielder Jo-Jo Moore, shortstop Dick Bartell, outfielder Mel Ott, catcher Gus Mancuso. Ott was with the Giants as player and manager from 1926 to 1948. He led in home runs six times, hit 511 overall, and batted .304.

Hank Leiber, outfielder with the Giants and Cubs from 1933 to 1942. Hank batted .331 for the Giants in 1935 and had a career average of .288.

Larry MacPhail.

Three Giant aces in 1937. Left to right: southpaws Carl Hubbell and Cliff Melton, and right-hander Hal Schumacher. Melton won 20 as a rookie in 1937, Schumacher won 23 in 1934.

Johnny Mize, one of the National League's most fearsome sluggers. Big John played with the Cardinals and Giants from 1936 to 1949, then was waived to the Yankees. In 11 National League seasons he hit better than .300 nine times, with a .364 peak in 1937. He led in batting in 1939 with .349 and in home runs four times, including 51 in 1947.

Dodger skipper Casey Stengel in 1936.

Jim Turner, a thirty-four-year-old rookie right-hander who won 20 for the Braves in 1937.

Lou Fette, Boston's other rookie 20-game winner in 1937.

Harry ("the Horse") Danning, Giant catcher from 1933 to 1942. Harry's career average is .285.

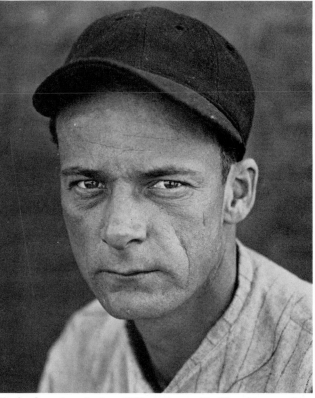

Right-hander Luke ("Hot Potato") Hamlin, a 20-game winner for the Dodgers in 1939, by far his best season.

At Brooklyn's Clearwater, Florida, spring training camp in March 1937 are (left to right) first baseman Buddy Hasset, Van Lingle Mungo, and Manager Burleigh Grimes.

The Cubs' pennant-winning infield in 1938. Left to right: Rip Collins, Billy Herman, Billy Jurges, Stan Hack.

Cub ace Bill Lee. Bill was 20–6 for the Cubs in 1935 and 22–9 in 1938. With the Cubs from 1934 to 1942, he later pitched for the Phillies and Braves, retiring in 1947 with a 169–157 lifetime record.

Mace Brown, the man who served up Hartnett's homer. Brown was a fine relief pitcher with the Pirates from 1935 to 1941, when he was traded to Brooklyn. He finished up with the Red Sox in 1946.

Gabby Hartnett moments after hitting his famous "homer in the gloamin'," September 28, 1938.

Outfielder Johnny Rizzo came up with the Pirates in 1938 and played five years in the National League with four teams.

Left to right: Cincinnati Manager Bill McKechnie, Johnny Vander Meer, and catcher Ernie Lombardi.

Johnny Vander Meer at work on his second-straight no-hitter at Ebbets Field on the night of June 15, 1938.

Cardinal Manager Ray Blades (left) shaking hands with his top hitter, Joe Medwick, in 1939.

Debs Garms, National League batting champion in 1940 with a .355 average. Debs was with the Pirates then. He came to the National League with the Braves in 1937 and finished up with the Cardinals in 1945.

Don Padgett, catcher and outfielder with the Cardinals and three other clubs from 1937 to 1948. Playing in 92 games for the Cardinals in 1939, Padgett hit a lofty .399.

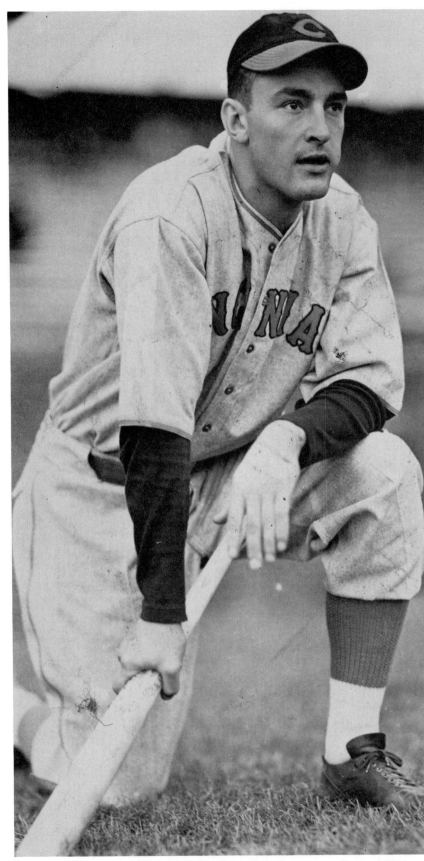

Harry Craft, Cincinnati's superb defensive center fielder on its pennant winners in 1939–1940. Harry played for the Reds from 1937 to 1942.

Frank McCormick, Cincinnati's fine first baseman from 1937 to 1945. He also played for the Phillies and Braves, retiring in 1948. Frank batted over .300 seven times and has a lifetime mark of .299.

Cincinnati catcher Ernie Lombardi showing off the size of his hand. Ernie came up with the Dodgers in 1931, was traded the next year to Cincinnati, and remained there until 1941. He later played for the Braves and Giants, retiring in 1947. Ernie batted over .300 ten times and took batting titles in 1938 and 1942, the only catcher other than Bubbles Hargrave to win a batting crown. His career average is .306.

Pirates Manager Pie Traynor with rookie infielder Frank Gustine in 1939. Frank played with Pittsburgh until 1948.

Paul Derringer, the other half of Cincinnati's awesome pitching duo. Paul came up with the Cardinals in 1931 and was traded to the Reds in 1933. A four-time 20-game winner with the Reds, he was traded to the Cubs in 1943 and finished up in 1945. His career record is 223–212.

Ival Goodman, solid-hitting Cincinnati outfielder from 1935 to 1942. Goodman led in triples his first two years. Lifetime average: .281.

Bucky Walters, the National League's best pitcher in 1939 and 1940, winning 27 and then 22 and leading both years in ERA and complete games. Converted by the Phillies from an infielder to a pitcher in 1935, he joined the Reds in 1938 and pitched for them until 1948, when he became manager. Lifetime record: 198–160.

Merrill ("Pinky") May, Phillie third baseman from 1939 to 1943.

Elbie Fletcher, a first baseman with a slick glove and snappy line-drive bat with the Braves and Pirates from 1934 to 1949. Elbie batted .271 lifetime.

Right-hander Hugh Mulcahy, a good pitcher with losing Phillies teams from 1935 to 1946. Hugh's lifetime 45–89 record does not reflect his abilities.

Vince DiMaggio, oldest of the three ballplaying Di-Maggio brothers, spent ten years in the National League with five clubs, from 1937 to 1946. Although he occasionally stroked the long ball (he drove in 100 runs with 21 homers for the Pirates in 1941), Vince was more noted for his strikeouts, leading the league in this department six times.

Braves outfielder Max West taking his cut in spring training in 1939. Max joined the Braves in 1938 and supplied what little punch the club had over the next few years.

Joe Beggs, who worked out of the bullpen for the 1940 Cincinnati pennant winners, winning 12 and losing 3. Joe pitched for the Reds until 1947, finishing up with the Giants a year later.

"Fiddler Bill" McGee, right-hander with the Cardinals and Giants from 1935 to 1942.

Johnny Rucker, speed merchant Giant outfielder from 1940 to 1946.

Norman ("Babe") Young, power-hitting first baseman with the Giants, Reds, and Cardinals from 1936 to 1948. Babe drove in over 100 for the Giants in 1940 and 1941.

Bobby Bragan, catcher and infielder with the Phillies and Dodgers from 1940 to 1948; later a brilliant and innovative manager of three big-league teams.

Leo Durocher in 1941.

6

Changing World, Changing Game

There was a force loose in the National League universe called Larry MacPhail. Brash, tempestuous, innovative, brilliant, MacPhail irritated everyone—his fellow club officials, the press, his managers, sometimes his players, but never the fans. Larry had taken a moribund Cincinnati club and in a few years seen it rise to pennant-winning heights in 1939–1940. By this time he was in Brooklyn, weaving the same magic.

The Brooklyn franchise was heavily in debt when MacPhail was induced to sign on as general manager in 1938. Spending wildly and predicting expansively, Larry promised long-suffering Dodger fans a winner. He installed lights in Ebbets Field and Leo Durocher as manager, and which shone brighter is hard to say. Leo was as brash and abrasive—and in his element as brilliant—as his boss. The two men clashed continually, with Leo constantly being "fired" and rehired.

Durocher, whose career as a light-hitting, superbly fielding shortstop was just coming to an end, was made for New York as no athlete since Ruth had been. Flashy, quick-witted, impeccably tailored, he loved the bright lights and attendant celebrities of the Big Town. The irrepressible Durocher hurled insults at the opposition, ordered beanballs, provoked brawls, and altogether made the Dodgers the most rambunctious, disliked club in the league. But MacPhail had spent lavishly and given Leo and Brooklyn a tough, exciting team that played their skipper's brand of ball.

In June 1940 MacPhail acquired from St. Louis the league's premier socker, Joe Medwick. To get Joe, Larry had to crack the vaults for $125,000, an impressive piece of change in those days. A week after he joined the Dodgers, Medwick was beaned so severely at Ebbets Field by ex-teammate Bob Bowman that Joe was never the same hitter again. The sight of his huge investment being so unceremoniously dented at home plate sent MacPhail into apoplexy. Larry threatened legal action against Bowman, insisted the pitcher be banned from baseball for life, and so forth. None of these dire happenings materialized and life went on in Brooklyn, with rising hysteria provided by fans who began sniffing their first winner since 1920.

Larry, always a man on the move, went out and obtained catcher Mickey Owen from the Cardinals, first baseman Dolf Camilli and pitcher Kirby Higbe from the Phillies, second baseman Billy Herman from the Cubs, shortstop Pee Wee Reese from the Red Sox farm system, and signed center fielder Pete Reiser, the jewel of the Cardinal organization, whom Judge Landis had declared a free agent in 1938. Along with American League castoffs Whit Wyatt, who became the team's ace, and outfielder Dixie Walker, this club brawled its way to the pennant in 1941, led by young Reiser's league-leading .343 average.

In 1942 it looked like the Dodgers again. The club was riding a ten-game lead in mid-August when MacPhail invaded the clubhouse one day and accused them of complacency, warning them that the young St. Louis team in second place was not giving up. Some of his players offered to bet Larry they would come in no less than eight games ahead of the Cardinals.

But Larry was right. The Cardinals, putting on the greatest stretch drive in history, won 43 of their final 51 games, overtook the Dodgers, and won by two. The Cardinals won 106 games to the Dodgers' 104.

The Dodger defeat could be attributed to an injury suffered in July by Reiser. The twenty-three-year-old flash, called by many the greatest natural ballplayer of all time—he could switch-hit, play infield or outfield, hit scorching line drives, and outrun anything on two feet—was ripping the ball at a .390 pace when he made violent contact with the concrete wall in Sportsman's Park in St. Louis while trying to run down a fly ball. "Pistol Pete" was never the same. Durocher returned him to the lineup prematurely and Pete, suffering from headaches and dizzy spells for the rest of the season, saw his average shrink to .310 and a sure Dodger pennant fritter away.

The St. Louis farm system was now producing star players faster and more abundantly than the big team could field them. Twenty-four of the club's 25-man roster in 1942 were products of the far-flung farm system, while the rest of the league was sprinkled with other Cardinal products who had been sold off by Rickey. (Supposedly Rickey received 25 percent of the sale price of any player he sold.)

Highlighting this dynasty, which was to take four pennants in five years, were pitchers Mort Cooper, Johnny Beazley, Ernie White, Howie Pollett, and Max Lanier. Mort's brother Walker was behind the plate. Shortstop Marty Marion was peerless on defense. In the outfield were Terry Moore, Enos Slaughter, and a slim left-handed hitter named Stan Musial, who had begun his baseball career as a lefty pitcher and switched to the outfield after suffering a sore arm.

Musial, the league's dominant hitter for more than a decade, was an immensely likable, modest, self-effacing man. He hit line drives that dug up divots in the outfield, and did so with such force and frequency in one three-game series at Ebbets Field that the awed and admiring citizens of Brooklyn bestowed upon him the lasting nickname of "Stan the Man." So he became and so he remained, through a career of 22 years that saw him win seven batting titles, lead in hits six times, doubles eight times, triples five times, and slugging six times. In his rookie year of 1942 Stan batted .315 and thereafter kept his batting average well over .300 until 1959.

As the nation became more and more deeply involved in the war, there was some uncertainty about baseball's status. Early in 1942, however, President Roosevelt had re-affirmed the game's importance as a diversion and morale builder in these times of increasing stress. In a letter to Judge Landis, Roosevelt said, "I honestly feel that it would be best for the country to keep baseball going. There will be fewer people unemployed and everybody will work longer hours and harder than ever before. And that means that they ought to have a chance for recreation and for taking their minds off their work even more than before."

As more and more players were drafted or enlisted, the teams became patchwork affairs, put together with overage players, rejects from military service, and many who simply had no business wearing major-league uniforms. In 1944 Cincinnati sent to the mound for part of one inning a young left-hander who had not yet attained his sixteenth birthday, Joe Nuxhall. Joe was properly mauled but came back in later years to have a fine big-league career.

Although they lost many of their regulars to the armed services, the Cardinals, by sheer dint of numbers, were able to bring in from their farm clubs competent replacements in greater quantities than anyone else. Consequently, the Redbirds rolled to easy pennants in 1943 and 1944, making it three in a row, with Stan Musial lashing base hits with consummate ease, taking his first batting crown in 1943, with a .357 average. In 1945, with Musial in the navy, the Cubs edged in to win the last flag they would take for decades, beating out the Cardinals by three games. The Cubs were powered by first baseman Phil Cavarretta, the league's Most Valuable Player and also its batting champion, with a .355 average.

The batting highlight of the 1945 season was turned in by Boston's sharp-hitting outfielder Tommy Holmes. From June 6 through July 8 Holmes hit safely in 37 consecutive games, establishing a modern National League record.

In November 1944 Judge Landis died, and in April 1945 big-league club owners in both leagues elected a new commissioner. He was a former governor and United States senator from Kentucky, Albert Benjamin ("Happy") Chandler. Chandler, a genial smooth-talking politico and baseball buff, who readily proclaimed, "Ah love baseball," was signed to a seven-year contract at $50,000 a year.

The war was over in August 1945 and the world was in for many changes, large and small, drastic and modest. The changes reached far and wide, even into the hitherto insular and immutable world of baseball. In October 1945 the Brooklyn Dodgers announced the signing of a player named Jackie Robinson, a move that sent the game reeling and began a social revolution that had been long, long overdue.

When Larry MacPhail went off to war in 1942, replacing him as head of the Dodgers was Branch Rickey. For years the thoughtful, erudite Rickey had been seething at a terrible injustice that no one seemed interested in correcting—the unwritten law against allowing blacks to play in organized ball. The blacks had their own leagues, they competed among themselves, and they participated in postseason exhibition games against white major leaguers. And they seemed content. But of course they were not. Year by year their great stars—and their best were the equal of any in the major leagues—watched with the quiet, aching bitterness of exclusion as organized ball continued to grow and expand, while they, players of the caliber of Satchel Paige and Josh Gibson and countless others, spent their prime years riding buses in and out of small towns and playing in rickety ball parks.

Branch Rickey had resolved decades before that he would see the color barrier in baseball broken down. He knew it would take time, and he knew it would take just the right man. The time came after the war, with the breaking or changing of so many hoary customs and traditions. And with the time came the man. The right man.

His name was Jackie Robinson. A superbly versatile athlete—he starred in baseball and football at UCLA—the twenty-six-year-old infielder was playing for the Kansas City Monarchs of the Negro American League when he was scouted and signed by the Brooklyn Dodgers and assigned for the 1946 season to their top farm club, Montreal, in the International League.

The story of Jackie Robinson is the story of baseball coming in out of the cold and becoming at last a fully participating member of American democracy. It is the story of a great athlete, a fierce competitor, a fiery outspoken militant, who because of what he was trying to do—integrate professional baseball without causing a racial incident—had to endure beanings, spikings, insults, provocations, death threats, ostracism, and countless humiliations with the pose of a stoic, to pretend that none of it was happening. No man has ever come to the big leagues under greater pressure than Jackie Robinson, and few men could have responded so tellingly. Using every ounce of the tremendous natural ability he possessed and motivating it with a passionate pride and relentless determination, he became the most exciting player of his era, and one of the greatest. A deadly clutch performer both at bat and in the field, he ran the bases with a boldness not seen, said old-timers, since the days of Ty Cobb. He became the heart and soul of a decade-long Brooklyn Dodger powerhouse, a symbol of baseball's coming of age, and for all time a pivotal figure in its history.

There was a reminder of old battles in 1946, when from Mexico came word that the Mexican multimillionaire Jorge Pascual was bankrolling a Mexican League to compete with the majors north of the border. In order to give his neophyte operation credibility, Pascual tried to hire away from the major leagues as many players as he could, using the old familiar method—money. Pascual succeeded in enticing away some top players, virtually all of them from the National League. The Giants lost seven players, including pitcher Sal Maglie and relief star Ace Adams. The Cardinals lost lefty Max Lanier after Max had compiled a 6–0 record for his first six starts, plus pitcher Fred Martin and infielder Lou Klein. The Dodgers lost their regular catcher, Mickey Owen, and outfielder Luis Olmo.

Commissioner Chandler met the challenge by laying down a very hard line. The jumpers, he decreed, would be barred from organized baseball—should they return—for five years. Owen, who returned in August, was the first to learn the commissioner meant business. Mickey, and the other returnees, most of them quickly disenchanted with the Mexican League, were not reinstated until 1949, when Chandler reinstated them.

The Dodgers and Cardinals picked up where they left off in 1942 and entertained the league with a sizzling pennant race. At the close of the 1946 season the two clubs were locked in a tie with identical 96–58 records, necessitating the first pennant play-off in big-league history, a best two-out-of-three series. Going at it in hand-to-hand combat, the Cardinals won in two straight, giving them their fourth flag in five years.

The Man was in full bloom now. Stan Musial hit .365 to lead the league and also led in doubles, triples, slugging, hits, runs, and total bases. Much to the dismay of National League pitchers, this was typical of the mayhem Stanley was going to cause for the next 15 years.

The home run leader in 1946, with a modest total of 23, was a twenty-three-year-old rookie outfielder with the Pirates, Ralph Kiner. A home run hitter in the classic mold—his blasts were generally high and far—Kiner went on to lead or tie for the home run title his first seven years, one of the most impressive records in distance hitting.

The following year the focus was largely on Brooklyn. It began in spring training when Commissioner Chandler suspended Brooklyn's colorful and controversial skipper Leo Durocher for a year. Chandler accused Leo of "conduct detrimental to baseball." The story was complicated. Larry MacPhail, by now running the New York Yankees, and Branch Rickey had engaged in some public name-calling. Leo joined the fray, using the forum of a ghost-written column in a Brooklyn newspaper. Leo and Rickey accused MacPhail of having entertained a couple of known gamblers in his box during a Yankee-Dodger exhibition game in Havana. The thing quickly got out of hand and Chandler, who seemed to harbor a dislike for Durocher, came down with the suspension, along with $2,000 fines each for the Dodgers and Yankees for sullying baseball's good name in public.

The suspension occurred about a week before the opening of the season. It was big news, but it was quickly overshadowed by something much more significant—the Dodgers' promotion of Jackie Robinson to their roster. Big-league baseball was now integrated. For Jackie, the lone black man on the scene at this point, it was a grueling season. Early on, some members of the St. Louis Cardinals were rumored to be threatening to strike rather than appear on the same field with the black man. National League President Ford C. Frick responded quickly and decisively with a threat of his own. Any player who struck, Frick said in a ringing statement, would be suspended. He did not care, Frick said, "if it wrecks the National League for five years. This is the United States of America and one citizen has as much right to play as another."

Frick's statement had a sobering effect. There was no strike; nevertheless, it was a hellish season for Robinson. Ignoring as best he could the taunts of the opposition, living with the resentment of some of his teammates, the first black man tore through the league like a tornado. He batted .297 and led the league with 29 stolen bases, helping drive the Dodgers to a pennant. The Brooklyn team was guided by the steady, patient hand of veteran Burt Shotton, brought in by Rickey to replace the suspended Durocher for the year.

What other noise was created in the league that year came from two noncontenders. Fifth-place Cincinnati put a beanpole right-hander named Ewell Blackwell on the mound, and the man with the wicked whiplash delivery had a 22–8 season that included 16 straight victories and a near-duplication of Johnny Vander Meer's double no-hitters. Blackie no-hit the Braves on June 18 and came within two outs of doing the same to Brooklyn in his next start, when second baseman Eddie Stanky grounded a single through Blackwell's legs into center field. The coincidences were many. Vander Meer's no-hitters had been against the same two clubs; and to top it off, Johnny, still with the Reds, was sitting in the dugout watching his teammate strive to attain this special immortality. "What was I thinking?" Vander Meer said in response to a question years later. "I was thinking that if he did it I wanted to be the first one out there to shake his hand."

The other noise, and it was thunderous, came from last-place Pittsburgh, where sophomore Ralph Kiner astounded everyone by launching 51 home runs, a figure matched by New York's veteran belter Johnny Mize. They were, after Hack Wilson, only the second and third men in National League history to top the 50 mark in home runs. Led by Mize, the Giants set a new home run record with 221. Behind Big John was Willard Marshall with 36, Walker Cooper with 35, and Bobby Thomson with 29. Despite all of this muscle, the team still finished fourth.

Leo Durocher was back at the helm of the Dodgers in 1948, but not for long. With the team playing .500 ball in July, and Leo squabbling with his players, Rickey finally tired of his controversial skipper and helped arrange the most startling managerial shift in all of baseball history. Fed up with a power-hitting but leaden-footed team that wasn't going anywhere, Giants owner Horace Stoneham was desperate to make a change. So he fired his long-time skipper and old Giant favorite, the quiet and likable Mel Ott (it was in reference to Ott that Leo made his famous pronouncement about nice guys finishing last) and hired the Dodger manager. It was a bitter pill for Giant fans to swallow, and even though Durocher brought them a pennant three years later, they were never entirely comfortable with him.

After a not overly impressive Boston Braves team, headed by righty Johnny Sain and lefty Warren Spahn, took the pennant in 1948, the Dodgers began in 1949 an eight-year stretch that saw them at or near the top in each of those years. In four of them the pennant wasn't decided until the final game of the season. This was Brooklyn-style baseball: strong, winning, tension-ridden.

The team put together by Branch Rickey is considered by some the greatest in National League history. With other clubs still reluctant to tap the rich pool of black talent, the Dodgers for several years had the pick of the crop. In addition to Robinson, they came away with catcher Roy Campanella and right-hander Don Newcombe. The Dodgers could also have had Larry Doby, but when Rickey learned that Cleveland's Bill Veeck wanted to sign the hard-hitting youngster and with him integrate the American League, Rickey stepped aside and let Doby go, saying that Veeck's pioneering was more important to what Rickey called "the cause" than the Dodgers adding another black player, talented as Doby was.

The Dodgers took the pennant in 1949 behind an electrifying MVP year by Robinson, who led the league with a .342 batting average. Jack also led in stolen bases with 37. If that seems like a modest total in light of what went on in later years, one should note that it

exceeded the team totals of the Reds, Braves, Phillies, and Cardinals.

Along with Robinson, Brooklyn's cast of regulars included Campanella, first baseman Gil Hodges, shortstop Pee Wee Reese (the last survivor of the 1941 pennant winners), third baseman Billy Cox, and outfielders Carl Furillo and Duke Snider. The club was young; it could hit and field and run and throw. If there was a weakness, it was on the mound, where the pitching was sometimes thin, although Brooklyn did have some outstanding hurlers in Newcombe, Preacher Roe, Carl Erskine, and Clem Labine.

After winning the pennant in the tenth inning of the last game of the season in Philadelphia (edging out a Cardinal team whose glory years were now behind them), the Dodgers followed the same pattern in 1950, but this time lost in the tenth inning of the last game of the season against the Phillies.

Actually, it should have been a cakewalk for Eddie Sawyer's young Philadelphia club, dubbed "the Whiz Kids." The Phillies had a seven-game lead with nine days to go. But then a pitching staff riddled by injuries and the September loss of ace lefty Curt Simmons to the army began showing its bare patches and the Whiz Kids went into a precipitous slide. In a schedule-maker's dream game, they met the Dodgers at Ebbets Field in the season's finale, one game up on Brooklyn.

For the third time in five games, Sawyer sent to the mound his ace, the brilliant, tireless right-hander Robin Roberts, ascending to greatness in his third National League season. With the sturdiness of an oak and the determination of a bulldog, the smooth-working Roberts matched Brooklyn's Don Newcombe pitch for pitch. It was a 1–1 tie going into the bottom of the ninth. The Dodgers threatened, putting men on first and second with none out. With the Phillies looking for a bunt, Duke Snider rifled a single to center. Center fielder Richie Ashburn raced in, scooped it up, and, making the peg of his life, nailed Dodger base runner Cal Abrams at the plate. In the top of the tenth, Dick Sisler hit a wrong-field, three-run shot into the lower stands in left, and the Phillies had their first pennant since 1915 and the days of Grover Cleveland Alexander, and Robin Roberts had the first of six consecutive 20-game seasons.

Elsewhere in the league, it was business as usual. Musial took another batting title, Kiner another home run title, and Warren Spahn won 21 games. The most impressive single-game batting feat was turned in by Brooklyn's Gil Hodges. On August 31 the muscular Dodger first baseman became the first National Leaguer in the twentieth century to hit four home runs in a game, when he unloaded against the Braves.

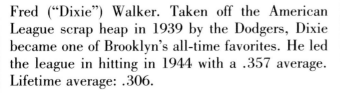

Fred ("Dixie") Walker. Taken off the American League scrap heap in 1939 by the Dodgers, Dixie became one of Brooklyn's all-time favorites. He led the league in hitting in 1944 with a .357 average. Lifetime average: .306.

Harold ("Pee Wee") Reese, Dodger shortstop from 1940 to 1958. Among twentieth-century National League shortstops, only Rabbit Maranville and Roy McMillan exceed Reese's 2,016 games at the position. Reese's lifetime average is .269.

Pistol Pete Reiser. Branch Rickey called him "the greatest ballplayer I ever saw."

Hugh Casey, ace Dodger relief pitcher from 1939 to 1948.

Dodger first baseman Dolf Camilli showing off the watch he was given as the National League's Most Valuable Player in 1941. Dolf came up with the Cubs in 1933, was traded to the Phillies a year later and then sold to Brooklyn in 1938. He led the league with 34 homers and 120 runs batted in, in 1941. His lifetime average is .277.

Another allegedly washed-up American Leaguer, Whitlow Wyatt joined the Dodgers in 1939 and pitched for them for six years. He was 22–10 in 1941 and 19–7 a year later.

Hard-throwing right-hander Kirby Higbe, 22–9 on the 1941 Dodger pennant winners. Higbe pitched in the National League from 1937 to 1950, with the Cubs, Phillies, Dodgers, Pirates, and Giants. Lifetime record: 118–101.

Elmer Riddle pitched for the Reds from 1939 to 1947 and then with Pittsburgh for two years. He was 19–4 in 1941 and 21–11 in 1943.

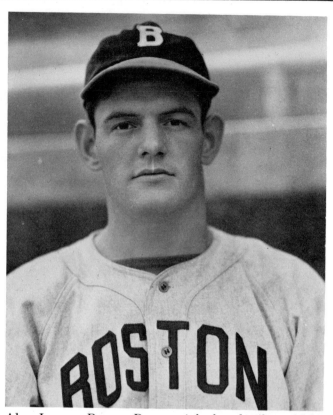

Shortstop Eddie Joost played with the Reds from 1936 to 1942, then with the Braves for two years, before going to the American League.

Alva Javery, Boston Braves right-hander from 1940 to 1946.

Clyde McCullough, Cub and Pirate catcher from 1940 to 1956.

Danny Litwhiler, outfielder with the Phillies, Cardinals, Braves, and Reds from 1940 to 1951. Danny batted .281 lifetime.

Catcher Walker Cooper, Mort's brother, came up with the Cardinals in 1940 and caught his brother on the 1942–1944 pennant winners. Walker played until 1957, appearing with every National League team except the Dodgers and Phillies. Six times a .300 hitter, his career average is .285.

Mort Cooper, ace Cardinal right-hander from 1938 to 1944. A 20-game winner for the Cards in 1942 through 1944, Mort later pitched for the Braves, Giants, and Cubs. Lifetime he was 128–75.

The Cardinals' "Mr. Shortstop" from 1940 to 1950, Marty Marion.

The Cardinals' crack outfield in 1942. Left to right: Stan Musial, Terry Moore, and Enos Slaughter. Peerless on defense, Moore was with the Cardinals from 1935 to 1948. Slaughter, a legendary nonstop hustler, was with the club from 1938 to 1953, batting .300 eight times.

Right-hander Johnny Beazley had a brilliant 21–5 rookie season for the Cardinals in 1942, went into the service, hurt his arm, and never regained his early brilliance.

Murry Dickson, a classy little right-hander who pitched in the National League with the Cardinals, Pirates, and Phillies from 1939 to 1957. He was a 20-game winner for a seventh-place Pirate club in 1951. Lifetime record: 172–181.

Ernie White, talented Cardinal left-hander from 1940 to 1943. Ernie was 17–7 in 1941, then saw his career aborted by a sore arm.

The Dodgers' Curt Davis pitching to the Cardinals' Johnny Mize at Ebbets Field in August 1941. The catcher is Mickey Owen, the umpire Tom Dunn.

Ace Adams, rubber-armed Giant relief pitcher from 1941 to 1946, when he jumped to the Mexican League. Ace led in games in 1942 through 1944.

Bill ("Swish") Nicholson, power-hitting outfielder with the Cubs and Phillies from 1939 to 1953. Bill had his best years with the Cubs, leading the National League in home runs and runs batted in, in 1943 and 1944. Lifetime average: .268.

Seven Dodger outfielders gathering for spring training in March 1943. Back row, left to right: Augie Galan, Paul Waner, Johnny Cooney, Frenchy Bordagaray. Front row, left to right: Dixie Walker, Joe Medwick, Luis Olmo.

Alpha Brazle, Cardinal southpaw from 1943 to 1954. Primarily a relief pitcher, he was 97–64 lifetime.

Right-hander George Munger, a hard thrower with the Cardinals from 1943 to 1952.

Four St. Louis Cardinals in 1943. Left to right: outfielder Harry Walker, third baseman George ("Whitey") Kurowski, second baseman Lou Klein, and Stan Musial.

Truett ("Rip") Sewell, inventor of the blooper ball, a soft, high-arcing pitch that he floated through the strike zone. Rip pitched for the Pirates from 1938 to 1949. He won 21 in each of the 1943 and 1944 seasons and has a 143–97 record lifetime.

Connie Ryan, National League second baseman from 1942 to 1954, playing with four clubs.

Outfielder-first baseman Johnny Hopp joined the Cardinals in 1939, was traded to the Braves in 1946, and later played for the Pirates and Dodgers. Johnny had five years over .300 and batted .296 lifetime.

Harry ("the Cat") Brecheen, fine Cardinal left-hander from 1943 to 1952. Harry sparkled in 1948 with a 20–7 record, leading in shutouts, ERA, and strikeouts. Lifetime record: 132–92.

Ted Wilks, Cardinal right-hander who turned in a fine 17–4 rookie season in 1944. He pitched for the Cards until 1951, when he was dealt to Pittsburgh.

Bill Voiselle, a big right-hander who pitched for the Giants from 1942 to 1947, later for the Braves and Cubs. Bill's big year was 1944, when he was 21–16.

Jim Tobin, right-hander for the Pirates and Braves from 1937 to 1944, winning 105 and losing 112. Jim could swing the bat, too; he hit three home runs in a game in 1942.

Harry ("Peanuts") Lowrey, outfielder with the Cubs, Reds, Cardinals, and Phillies from 1942 to 1955. Peanuts batted .273 lifetime.

Outfielder Andy Pafko, who had many good years with the Cubs, Dodgers, and Braves from 1943 to 1959. Lifetime average: .285.

Right-hander Charlie ("Red") Barrett. Red pitched for the Reds, Braves, and Cardinals from 1937 to 1949, with one big season in 1945, when he was 23–12.

Tommy Holmes, sharp-eyed, line-drive-hitting outfielder with the Braves from 1942 to 1951. Tommy batted .352 in 1945 and led with 28 home runs and 224 hits. His career average is .302.

Three New York Giants skipping off from Miami in April 1946 to join the newly formed Mexican League. Left to right: first baseman Roy Zimmerman, pitcher Sal Maglie, and second baseman George Hausmann.

Stylish was the word for left-hander Howie Pollett. He joined the Cardinals in 1941 and was a 20-game winner for them in 1946 and 1949. He later pitched for the Pirates and Cubs. His career mark is 131–116.

Albert ("Red") Schoendienst, classy second baseman with the Cardinals from 1945 to 1956, when he was traded to the Giants. Red later played on Milwaukee's pennant winners in 1957–1958, retiring in 1963, when he was back with the Cardinals. Red's top year was 1953, when he batted .342. Lifetime average: .289. Red managed the Cardinals from 1965 to 1976.

Johnny Schmitz, highly regarded left-hander with the Cubs in the 1940s.

John ("Buddy") Kerr, shortstop with the Giants and Braves from 1943 to 1951. Buddy could field with the best of them.

Grady Hatton, Cincinnati third baseman from 1946 to 1954.

Jackie Robinson.

Thunder over the Polo Grounds in 1947. Left to right: Walker Cooper, Johnny Mize, Willard Marshall. Their respective home run totals that year were 35, 51, 36.

Highly touted as a pitcher and power-hitting outfielder, Clint Hartung tried it both ways with the Giants from 1947 to 1952, never quite living up to his promise.

Ewell Blackwell. His great year was 1947, when he won 16 straight, ending up with a 22–8 record. Lifetime he was 82–78.

Rip Sewell testing the muscles of young home run hitter Ralph Kiner.

Long-time American League home run champ Hank Greenberg played his last big-league season with Pittsburgh in 1947. Here he is displaying a plaque he received on Hank Greenberg Day at the Polo Grounds on August 23, 1947.

Boston's top pitchers in 1948, Warren Spahn (left) and Johnny Sain. A four-time 20-game winner, Johnny won 24 that year.

A half dozen members of Boston's 1948 pennant winners. Left to right: Sibby Sisti, Frank McCormick, Earl Torgeson, Alvin Dark, Ed Stanky, Bob Elliott.

Vern Bickford, Braves pitcher from 1948 to 1953. A 19-game winner in 1950, his lifetime was 66–57.

Phil Masi, Boston Braves catcher from 1939 to 1949.

Eddie Miller, one of the finest fielding shortstops ever in the National League. Eddie played for four teams between 1936 and 1950.

Ken Raffensberger, a left-hander who pitched for four teams between 1939 and 1954. He had his best years for the Reds, for whom he worked from 1947 to 1954. Lifetime he was 119–154.

Pete Reiser and Branch Rickey in 1948. Pete is about to sign his contract.

Jackie Robinson stealing home against the Braves at Ebbets Field in August 1948. The catcher is Bill

Salkeld, the umpire Jocko Conlan. Moving aside is Dodger Billy Cox.

Gil Hodges, the Dodgers' great first baseman from 1947 to 1961. He finished up with the Mets, whom he later managed, in 1963. From 1949 to 1955, Gil had seven straight years of over 100 RBIs. Over his career he hit 370 home runs and batted .273.

Third baseman on three Dodger pennant winners, Billy Cox had no peer when it came to flashing a glove at the hot corner.

Obtained from Pittsburgh along with Billy Cox in 1948, Preacher Roe became Brooklyn's greatest southpaw since Nap Rucker. Roe, whose square name was Elwin, pitched for the Brooks from 1948 to 1954. In 1951 he was 22–3. Lifetime he stands at 127–84.

Roy Campanella, Dodger catcher from 1948 to 1957 and the league's Most Valuable Player in 1951, 1953, and 1955. An automobile accident in January 1958 ended his career and put him in a wheelchair for the rest of his life.

Carl Furillo, Dodger outfielder from 1946 to 1960. A solid hitter with a powerful throwing arm, Carl led the league with a .344 batting average in 1953. Lifetime average: .299.

Don Newcombe, ace of the great Dodger teams from 1949 to 1957. Newk was 20–9 in 1951, 20–5 in 1955, 27–7 in 1956. Lifetime he was 149–90.

Duke Snider, Dodger center fielder from 1947 to 1962. A do-it-all player, Snider had career figures of 407 homers and .295 batting average.

Bob Rush, a big right-hander for the Cubs from 1948 to 1957, then with the Braves until 1960. Career record: 127–152.

Ted Kluszewski, Cincinnati's strongman first baseman from 1947 to 1957. Ted batted over .300 seven times, with a lifetime of .298. He hit 49 home runs in 1954, 47 the next year.

Del Rice, Cardinal catcher from 1945 to 1955, then with the Braves and Cubs.

A young battery with a great future. Del Crandall (left) caught for the Braves from 1949 to 1963. Southpaw Johnny Antonelli went on to have his best seasons for the Giants, winning 21 in 1954 and 20 in 1956.

Sam Jethroe, fleet-footed outfielder with the Braves in the early 1950s. He led in stolen bases in 1950 and 1951.

Bill Rigney, Giant infielder from 1946 to 1953. He later managed the club.

Herman Wehmeier, right-hander with the Reds, Phillies, and Cardinals from 1945 to 1958. He was 92–108 lifetime.

Robin Roberts, Phillie ace from 1948 to 1961. He won 20 or more six straight seasons, from 1950 through 1955, peaking with a 28–7 record in 1952. After leaving the Phillies he pitched for Baltimore, then returned to the National League and finished up with the Cubs in 1966. Lifetime record: 286–245.

Part of the National League's attack for the 1949 All-Star Game at Ebbets Field. Left to right: Jackie Robinson, Ralph Kiner, Red Schoendienst, Willard Marshall.

Granny Hamner, Phillie shortstop from 1944 to 1959.

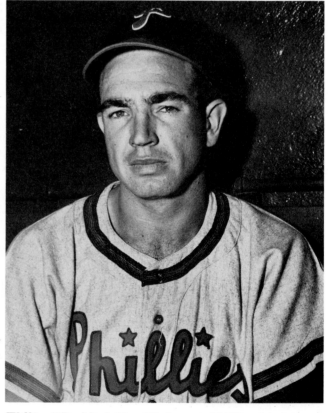

Willie ("Puddin' Head") Jones, Phillie third baseman from 1947 to 1959.

Del Ennis, power man on the 1950 Phillies. Del played from 1946 to 1959, mostly for the Phillies. He drove in over 100 runs seven times and batted .285 lifetime.

Jim Konstanty, ace relief pitcher for the Phillies in 1950. Jim won 16 and saved 22. He was voted MVP that year.

Richie Ashburn had his best years for the Phillies, for whom he played from 1948 to 1959, later playing for the Cubs and Mets before retiring in 1962. Richie led the league in batting in 1955 with a .338 average and again in 1958 with a .350 mark. He hit over .300 nine times and .308 for his career.

Dick Sisler, the man whose home run gave the Phillies the 1950 pennant. Dick played for the Cardinals, Phillies, and Reds from 1946 to 1953.

The Phillies' clubhouse moments after the clinching of the 1950 pennant at Ebbets Field.

Willie Mays in 1951.

7

The Dodgers: Brooklyn and Los Angeles

When he took over the Giants in 1948, Leo Durocher found a team with a lot of power but very little running speed. Leo wasn't comfortable with this kind of club and set out to tear down and rebuild the Giants in his own image. Accordingly, he began dealing away his big sluggers. By 1951 Mize, Cooper, Marshall, and Sid Gordon were gone. The key transaction occurred with the Braves, from whom the Giants obtained shortstop Alvin Dark and second baseman Eddie Stanky for Marshall, Gordon, and shortstop Buddy Kerr.

Leo opened the 1951 season brimming with confidence. His infield was Monte Irvin on first base, Stanky at second, Dark at short, and Henry Thompson alternating with Bobby Thomson at third. In the outfield he had Thomson, Whitey Lockman, and Don Mueller. After about a month, Leo moved Irvin to the outfield and put Lockman on first. On the mound he had a trio of strong right-handed starters in Sal Maglie, back from Mexico in 1950 and an immediate winner with an 18–4 record; Larry Jansen; and Jim Hearn. Leo's lefty starter was Dave Koslo, and he had an effective bullpen operative in sinkerball specialist George Spencer.

The Giants ran into early-season miseries, however, suffered an 11-game losing streak, and watched Charlie Dressen's Dodgers run up what eventually seemed an insurmountable lead. In the face of all reason and logic, however, the Giants refused to quit. Much of the spirit that infused the Giants in that memorable year was contributed by the twenty-year-old center fielder they brought up from their Minneapolis farm club in late May, Willie Mays.

Young Mays could do it all, and then some. The youngster not only possessed all of the classic requirements of super stardom—hitting, hitting with power, running, throwing, fielding—but went about his daily labors with an uninhibited joyousness that was infectious. Willie bubbled and giggled and laughed, and he hit home runs, ran out from under his cap in making impossible catches, and made eye-popping throws from the outfield. With Willie in center, Leo's team was set. The only problem lay in trying to overhaul the powerful, high-flying Dodgers.

On August 12 the Giants' task seemed an impossibility. The second-place New Yorkers were 13½ games behind. But then, lashed and goaded and cajoled by Durocher, they ran off a 16-game winning streak. They kept going, winning 39 of their last 47 games, whittling away remorselessly at the Brooklyn bulge. On the last day of the season both clubs were locked in a dead heat. The Giants won their game in Boston, while the Dodgers had to struggle in extra innings to beat the Phillies on the strength of Jackie Robinson's home run, forcing a play-off.

The Giants won the first game at Ebbets Field. The Dodgers returned the favor the next day at the Polo Grounds, winning behind rookie Clem Labine's 10–0 shutout. The stage was set for "the game of the century."

It was a match-up of aces, Brooklyn's Newcombe and New York's Maglie. The Dodgers carried a 4–1 lead into the bottom of the ninth, whereupon the Giants launched a rally that typified the brand of ball they had been playing for six weeks. Dark opened with a single to right. Mueller rolled a seeing-eye hit through the same side. Giant hopes rose, Dodger hopes faltered. Newcombe, who had pitched heroically the past week, retired Irvin on a pop foul. But then Lockman poked a double down the left-field line, scoring one run and putting the tying runs on second and third. At this point the weary Newcombe left and right-hander Ralph Branca came in to face Bobby Thomson.

Branca threw a strike. Then he wound up

and threw another strike, but this time Thomson hit it. The ball flew on a line to left field, cleared the head of leftfielder Andy Pafko, cleared the wall, and disappeared into the lower stands. The Polo Grounds erupted; Giant fans went into a frenzy, Dodger fans stared with frozen faces, and the single-most dramatic and legendary moment in baseball history had been born.

Many teams would have been broken and demoralized by losing a pennant under such heartbreaking circumstances. The Dodgers, however, came roaring back to take the next two pennants, despite the loss of their ace Don Newcombe to the army. Compensating for Newk's loss in 1952 was a fast-balling right-handed rookie relief pitcher named Joe Black, who gave the club a phenomenal 15–4 season that included 15 saves. Black never came close to repeating his remarkable 1952 year, but there is no question he was the difference between first and second place for Brooklyn that season.

The Giants also unveiled a rookie relief pitcher in 1952 who was in many ways the direct antithesis of Black. His name was Hoyt Wilhelm and, like Black, at twenty-eight a rather mature rookie. Where Black relied on speed, Wilhelm threw, pitch after maddening pitch, a knuckle ball that cavorted like a butterfly on a lazy summer's day. The pitch was not only almost unhittable but also almost uncatchable, to the extent that his bullpen catchers often donned a mask when getting Wilhelm ready. Where Black had a relatively short career, Wilhelm went on to one of the longest pitching careers in big-league history, throwing his butterfly for 21 years in a record 1,070 games, not retiring until 1972, when he was forty-nine.

In 1953 some of the ties that bind began coming loose. For the first time since 1903 there was a franchise shift in the National League, the Boston Braves giving up the ghost and moving to Milwaukee. Boston had always been a Red Sox town anyway, and the Braves had been looked upon as poor cousins, generally with teams that warranted fan indifference. Since 1901 the Braves had won just two pennants and finished in the second division 40 times. In 1952 they had drawn 281,000 customers, creating more echoes than cheers in old Braves Field.

The move to Milwaukee proved that a change of address and a new suit of clothes could do wonders. Cheered on by an astounding 1,820,000 fans, the Braves elevated themselves to second place. Warren Spahn, getting better with age, was 23–7, while the big buster in the lineup was sophomore third baseman Eddie Mathews. The twenty-one-year-old strongboy suddenly became a dominant home run hitter with a league-leading 47, ending Ralph Kiner's seven-year reign at the top of the four-bagger club. Ralph, in fact, was outgunned that year by not only Mathews but also Brooklyn's Duke Snider and Roy Campanella and Cincinnati's mountain of muscles Ted Kluszewski.

The Braves' financial success in Milwaukee was to prove significant. The minds of club owners whose teams were struggling at the gate began turning to greener pastures. The era of franchise shifting and ultimately of expansion had begun. What had once been considered sacrosanct—the idea of a team being rooted forever like concrete in a city—was now beginning to undergo some serious rethinking.

The Dodgers' march toward a third-straight pennant in 1954 was roadblocked by Durocher's Giants, rejuvenated by the return from military service of Willie Mays and the acquisition from the Braves of left-hander Johnny Antonelli in a swap for pennant hero Bobby Thomson. Willie the Wonder hit 41 home runs and led the league with a .345 batting average, edging out teammate Don Mueller and Duke Snider on the last day of the season. Antonelli, a hard thrower to whom the Braves had paid a handsome signing bonus in 1948, suddenly blossomed with a 21–7 record.

Managing the second-place Dodgers in 1954 was a new face. It belonged to an organization man who had had just one time at bat in the big leagues (he struck out). His name was Walter Alston and he was replacing Charlie Dressen, who had demanded a three-year contract from Dodger owner Walter O'Malley as a reward for winning two straight pennants. O'Malley was reluctant to show such faith in a manager and when Dressen couched the demand in the form of an ultimatum, he was canned. When Alston failed to deliver an expected pennant in 1954, it was assumed that he, too, would get the boot. But O'Malley stood fast behind his rookie skipper, and when Alston finally did leave the Dodgers, it was 23 years later in a place called Los Angeles.

There were some notable slugging achievements in 1954. On May 2 Stan Musial thrilled the hometown fans in St. Louis by smashing five home runs in a doubleheader against the Giants and establishing a new major-league record. On July 23 Milwaukee's big first baseman Joe Adcock hit four home runs in a game against the Dodgers at Ebbets Field. And on April 23, in an event that attracted little attention, a Milwaukee rookie named Henry Aaron tagged the Cardinal's Vic Raschi for his first big-league home run.

In 1955 the Dodgers settled the issue early and decisively by winning 22 of their first 24 games. They were 9½ games in front after a month of play. They kept going, clinching the pennant on September 8, the earliest date ever for a pennant celebration in National League history. Powering the Dodgers, who hit 201 home runs, were Roy Campanella, who walked away with his third MVP Award, RBI leader Duke Snider, Gil Hodges, Carl Furillo, Jackie Robinson, and Pee Wee Reese. Don Newcombe led the pitchers with a 20–5 record.

The National League had now become baseball's power center. Along with the

Dodger clubbers were Mays with 51 home runs, Kluszewski with 47, Mathews with 41, and a young shortstop with the Cubs named Ernie Banks, who had a whiplash swing and put away 44. Young Henry Aaron had his first big season, batting .314, hitting 27 homers, and driving in 106 runs. In Pittsburgh the Pirates unveiled a twenty-year-old outfielder named Roberto Clemente. A bundle of proud, brooding, simmering talent, Clemente, who had been drafted from the Dodger organization for a mere $10,000, opened up quietly, batting just .255. The Dodgers had left the youngster exposed to the draft at Montreal in 1954, realized their mistake, and were praying no one would claim him. But a canny Pittsburgh scout named Clyde Sukeforth, on assignment to check out another player, saw Clemente, and what he saw made his eyes pop and his head spin. By finishing last in 1954 the Pirates were entitled to first pick in the draft. The man they selected was Clemente, a man destined to write a chapter in Pirate history to match those of Honus Wagner, Paul Waner, and Ralph Kiner.

A rules change of some significance was made by league directors at their annual winter clambake. By a vote of 6 to 2 they made it compulsory for all players to wear a protective helmet when batting. One has to wonder if the two who voted against the proposal ever stood at home plate against a fast baller with less-than-perfect control.

For the fourth time in eight years, the Dodgers took the pennant race down to the last day of the season, this time staving off the challenges of the Reds, who were eliminated a few days before the end of the season, and the Braves, who stayed in it until the final day. Needing to win their game on the last day of the season against the Pirates, the Dodgers sewed it up when Don Newcombe hurled his twenty-seventh victory.

The Braves had now become a formidable challenger, powered by the home run bats of Aaron, Mathews, and Adcock, and led on the mound by Spahn and right-handers Lew Burdette and Bob Buhl, the latter with the precious knack of being able to beat the Dodgers. In 1956 the slim, quiet Aaron won the first of his two batting titles, with a .328 mark. The young man from Mobile had already evolved into the complete player, but because he did not play with the flamboyance of a Mays, he did not for many years receive the general fan appreciation that Willie did.

Cincinnati, tying the Giants' home run record with a club total of 221, had added another slugger to go along with the bombing done by Kluszewski, Wally Post, Gus Bell, and Ed Bailey. His name was Frank Robinson. He was a twenty-year-old Texan who broke into Cincinnati's outfield with a considerable bang, hitting 38 home runs, tying Wally Berger's 1930 major-league record for home runs by a rookie.

Robinson was in many ways symbolic of what was happening in the big leagues. The National League had pioneered the signing of black players; the American League had chosen to proceed more cautiously. As a consequence, most of the outstanding young black players were signing with National League clubs, because the Nationals were after them and because the blacks wanted to be on the same teams with players like Jackie Robinson, Willie Mays, and others. It was a pattern that was to continue for more than a decade, accounting in large measure for the National League's eventual dominance of its junior partner.

Though black players were now appearing in greater numbers in the American League, the National had performers like Aaron, Banks, Clemente, Bill White, Frank Robinson, and others to go along with the veterans Jackie Robinson, Campanella, Mays, Irvin, Newcombe. The American League could not come close to matching them.

Late in May in the 1956 season, Pittsburgh's Dale Long, a tall, power-hitting first baseman, took off on baseball's greatest consecutive-game home-run-hitting streak when he drove one out of the park for eight straight games until finally being stopped on May 29 by Newcombe.

In 1957 the Braves finally made it all the way to the top, finishing eight games ahead of the Cardinals as an aging Dodger team slipped to third place. For the Braves it was Spahn, Burdette, and Buhl on the mound, with Spahn a 20-game winner for the eighth time. At the plate it was all Henry Aaron, the twenty-three-year-old slugger turning his heavy cannons on the league all season long, putting together his first truly great year with 44 home runs and 132 runs batted in, giving him a dynamite-laden .322 batting average. The batting champion, however, for the seventh and last time, was the thirty-six-year-old Stan Musial, who set the standard with a .351 mark, the fifth time the St. Louis marvel had cleared .350 in his career. In National League history only Wagner, Hornsby, and Paul Waner have climbed that high that often.

The big news in the National League in 1957, however, did not take place on the diamond. On August 19 came the announcement that the directors of the New York Giants had by a vote of 8 to 1 decided to move the franchise to San Francisco. The reasons for the move were to become classic: declining attendance, an outmoded ball park in a deteriorating urban setting, inadequate parking facilities, and an opportunity to exploit virgin pastures, which looked very green indeed. When on September 29 the New York Giants played their last game ever at the Polo Grounds, they rang down the curtain on a tradition that had begun when New York joined the National League in 1883. The Giants' attendance had fallen to 650,000 in 1957, a figure they easily surpassed and often more than doubled in each of their first ten years in San Francisco.

On October 8 an announcement by the Brooklyn Dodgers confirmed the summer's most persistent rumor: the team was joining the trek westward, their destination Los Angeles. Actually, it was Brooklyn's Walter O'Malley, as shrewd and wily a man as ever owned a ball club, who conceived, planned, and engineered the way west for big-league baseball. Realizing that the league might not approve a single western outpost, O'Malley talked Giants owner Horace Stoneham into coming along. The Dodgers were suffering from each of the classic ills except poor attendance. On the contrary, Brooklyn had what were probably the most faithful and vociferous fans in baseball. O'Malley, however, was bewitched by the almost incalculable riches to be gained by planting a big-league club in one of the nation's most lush, rapidly expanding metropolitan areas. The O'Malley vision of the future proved to be crystal clear, as the Los Angeles Dodgers eventually became baseball's most successful franchise.

In their first season in Los Angeles, playing in a lopsided Los Angeles Memorial Coliseum that was ludicrously unfit for baseball, the Dodgers broke their Ebbets Field attendance record of 1,807,526 by nearly 40,000. The Giants played their games in the stadium hitherto used by the San Francisco Seals of the Pacific Coast League. In a park with a seating capacity of just under 23,000, the Giants drew 1,272,625 fans, 300,000 under the club's all-time record set in 1947.

These figures, along with the Braves' continuing success in Milwaukee, drove home the fact that all across the country were fans thirsting for major-league baseball. Club owners began wondering what baseball gold mines might lay in the South, the Midwest, the Southwest, the Pacific Northwest. If two of the game's most tradition-drenched clubs could leave New York, then there were no holds barred anywhere.

Despite the cheers ringing in their ears all season long, the best the transplanted Dodgers could manage was seventh place, while the Giants, behind Willie Mays' .347 batting average and some lusty hitting by

Rookie-of-the-Year Orlando Cepeda, finished third, 12 games behind the repeating Braves. There were three 20-game winners in the league that year and Milwaukee had two of them—the perennial Warren Spahn and Lew Burdette (Pittsburgh's Bob Friend was the third). The MVP Award went to Chicago's stellar shortstop Ernie Banks, hitting like an outfielder with 47 home runs, a record for a shortstop.

The league put on a real scramble of a pennant race in 1959. The principals were the defending Braves, the Giants, and the Dodgers. With a week to go, the Giants led by two games. When they began to falter, however, the Braves and the Dodgers kept coming, finally passing the Giants and ending in a deadlock at the close of the season, forcing a play-off for the pennant. It was the third play-off in National League history, and each time the Dodgers had been involved.

The Dodgers took the opener of the best two-out-of-three series in Milwaukee and the teams went to Los Angeles for the second and, if necessary, third games. The third game was not necessary, as the Dodgers staged a heroic three-run rally in the bottom of the ninth to tie the game and then won it in the bottom of the twelfth inning. For the transplanted Brooklyns (as many of their back-east fans still referred to them) it was a remarkable comeback from their seventh-place finish in 1958.

Ernie Banks put together another titanic season with 45 home runs and 143 runs batted in to earn him his second consecutive MVP Award. Henry Aaron, pounding away year after year now with monotonous splendor, won the batting championship with a .355 average, the highest he ever hit in his career. Spahn and Burdette again won 20 games; for the thirty-eight-year-old Spahn, rapidly becoming a geriatric wonder on the mound, it was the tenth time he entered this charmed circle of pitching.

The story of the year in the National League was written on May 26 at Milwaukee by a slightly built Pittsburgh lefty named Harvey Haddix. For most of his 14-year career little better than a .500 pitcher, the thirty-four-year-old southpaw was on May 26, 1959, the greatest pitcher who ever lived, pitching a dream game far beyond anything ever seen before.

Working against the league's hardest-hitting lineup, an array that included Aaron, Mathews, Adcock, Del Crandall, Johnny Logan, Andy Pafko, and Wes Covington, Haddix curve-balled through 12 perfect innings, an absolutely unprecedented and astonishing feat. Unfortunately for Harvey, he was matched this night by Lew Burdette, and while Lew scattered hits all night, he let no one score. After retiring the first 36 Milwaukee batters he saw, Harvey had his first man reach base in the bottom of the thirteenth, when third baseman Don Hoak made a bad throw on a grounder hit by Felix Mantilla. Working out of a stretch for the first time, Haddix saw Mathews sacrifice Mantilla to second. Aaron was purposely walked. Adcock then lofted a ball over the fence in right center. What should have been a home run was ruled a double after some base-running blunders by the Braves, but Mantilla was entitled to score and Haddix went home that night with baseball's greatest-ever pitched game and a 1–0 defeat. As remarkable as Harvey's game was, a question reportedly put to him in a postgame interview by a young sports writer is equally memorable. "Harvey," the young man in full earnest asked, "was this the greatest game you ever pitched?"

In 1960, a poker-faced Irishman named Danny Murtaugh led the Pirates to their first pennant in 33 years. Pittsburgh had some outstanding talents, notably a defensive magician named Bill Mazeroski at second, batting champion Dick Groat at short, and the incomparable Clemente in right field. A mound staff topped by 20-game winner Vernon Law and Bob Friend was propped up by a 5'8" relief ace named Elroy Face.

In Los Angeles the Dodgers finished fourth. There was nothing particularly impressive about the club that year, nor did too many people pay much attention to a twenty-four-year-old left-hander who compiled a forgettable 8–13 record that year. Some of the young man's statistics bore a closer look, however. Twenty-four pitchers in the league pitched more innings than his 175, but only one—teammate Don Drysdale—struck out more than Sandy Koufax's 197. Koufax was at the top of the charts in allowing the least hits per nine innings—6.84. In other words, when the young southpaw was getting the ball over the plate, they weren't hitting it. His problem was control—he walked 100 men. To most baseball fans Sandy Koufax was merely an 8–13 pitcher; to National League hitters muttering as they dragged their bats back to the dugout, he was potentially the toughest pitcher in the league.

Henry Thompson, Giant third baseman from 1949 to 1956. He was a .267 lifetime hitter.

Giants Whitey Lockman, Bobby Thomson, and Don Mueller in 1952.

Celebrating a victory over the Dodgers at Ebbets Field in the early 1950s are (left to right) Alvin Dark, Monte Irvin, Wes Westrum, and Willie Mays.

Sal Maglie. Sal returned from the Mexican League in 1950 and was 18–4, then was 23–6 the following year. He pitched for the Giants until 1955. A year later his 13–5 record helped the Dodgers to the pennant. The curve-balling "Barber" (so called for the close shaves he gave batters) was 119–62 lifetime.

Larry Jansen, 21–5 in his 1947 rookie year with the Giants and 23–11 in the 1951 "miracle" year. Larry pitched for the Giants until 1954. Lifetime record: 122–89.

Dave Koslo, a steady lefty with the Giants from 1941 to 1952. Dave was 92–107 for his career.

Four ex-Dodgers a day after they were traded to the Cubs. Left to right: pitcher Joe Hatten, infielder Eddie Miksis, catcher Bruce Edwards, outfielder Gene Hermanski. The deal was made in June 1951.

A familiar sight: Manager Leo Durocher cheering a Willie Mays home run.

Ralph Branca. Ralph was with the Dodgers from 1944 to 1953. A hard-throwing right-hander, he won 21 in 1947. In 1951 he made one pitch too many.

Joe Black. One great year.

Bobby Thomson and the Miracle Moment on October 3, 1951.

Timber time in Brooklyn. Left to right: Duke Snider, Gil Hodges, Jackie Robinson, Pee Wee Reese, Roy Campanella.

Four Brooklyn Dodgers celebrating a victory. Left to right: pitcher Clem Labine, second baseman Jim Gilliam, Duke Snider, and pitcher Billy Loes.

Carl Erskine, classy Dodger right-hander from 1948 to 1959. He was 20–6 in 1953, 122–78 lifetime.

Hoyt Wilhelm. He began with the New York Giants in 1952 and ended with the Los Angeles Dodgers at the age of forty-nine in 1972. He pitched for nine teams in both leagues and appeared in a record 1,070 games. Lifetime record: 143–122.

A view of Ebbets Field as the Dodgers and Yankees line up for game three of the 1953 World Series.

Davey Williams, Giant second baseman from 1949 to 1955.

Dee Fondy, first baseman with the Cubs, Pirates, and Reds from 1951 to 1958. He was a lifetime .286 hitter.

Stanky has just fed to Dark, who is firing to first to complete a double play. The man in the dirt is Sam Jethroe.

Mainstays of the Phillies' 1952 pitching staff. Left to right: Robin Roberts, Curt Simmons, Karl Drews.

There are 17 bats between these three Milwaukee hitters. Left to right: Eddie Mathews, Bill Bruton, and Sid Gordon.

Five Cardinal chuckers staring down the camera in spring training 1953. Left to right: Harvey Haddix, Stu Miller, Gerry Staley, Cliff Chambers, Wilmer ("Vinegar Bend") Mizell.

Hank Sauer, National League MVP with the Cubs in 1952, when he hit 37 homers and drove in 121 runs. He hit 30 or more homers six times.

Roy McMillan. There was never a better glove at shortstop. Roy played for the Reds from 1951 to 1960, then with the Braves and Mets until 1966.

Outfielder Jim Greengrass, who turned in some heavy stickwork for the Reds and Phillies from 1952 to 1956.

Ruben Gomez, Giant right-hander from 1953 to 1958. Ruben's best was 17–9 in 1954.

Forrest ("Smoky") Burgess, National League catcher with four clubs from 1949 to 1964. Smoky swung a sharp bat, hitting .368 for the Phillies in 1954 and .295 lifetime.

Johnny Temple, Cincinnati second baseman from 1952 to 1959. He cleared .300 three times for the Reds.

A familiar ritual: Stan Musial getting a silver bat for winning a batting championship. It's May 1953. Doing the honors is National League President Warren Giles.

Milwaukee Braves rookie Henry Aaron in 1954.

Third baseman Ray Jablonski, who knocked in over 100 runs in his first two seasons with the Cardinals, 1953–1954.

Frank Thomas, outfielder with seven National League teams from 1951 to 1966. His best years were with Pittsburgh, from 1951 to 1958. Lifetime average: .266.

Ed Bailey, power-hitting catcher with the Reds in the 1950s.

Gus Bell, hard-hitting out-fielder with the Pirates, Reds, Mets, and Braves from 1950 to 1964. His top years were with the Reds from 1953 to 1961. His career average is .281.

Frank Robinson.

Wally Post, another Cincinnati powerhouse of the 1950s. Wally hit 40 homers in 1955, 36 the next year.

Roberto Clemente in 1955.

Eddie Mathews and Henry Aaron.

Brooks Lawrence, right-hander with the Cardinals and Reds from 1954 to 1960. He won 19 for the Reds in 1956.

Johnny Logan, shortstop on Milwaukee's pennant winners in 1957 and 1958.

Three Pirate pitchers in 1956. Left to right: Ron Kline, Bob Friend, Elroy Face.

Juan Pizarro, a smoke thrower the Braves brought up in 1957. Juan was around for 18 years, pitching for seven teams in both leagues.

Joe Adcock, Milwaukee's slugging first baseman through most of the 1950s. A big leaguer for 17 years, Joe hit 336 home runs and batted .277.

Right-hander Lew Burdette pitched in the National League from 1951 to 1965 before finishing up in the American League. Lew's glory years were with the Braves from 1953 to the early 1960s. He was a 20-game winner in 1958–1959 and was 203–144 for his career.

Lindy McDaniel, 21 years a big leaguer. Lindy was in the National League with the Cardinals, Cubs, and Giants from 1955 to 1968. Primarily a relief pitcher, he worked in 987 games, second only to Hoyt Wilhelm, ending with a 141–119 record.

Larry Jackson, a real professional on the mound for the Cardinals, Cubs, and Phillies from 1955 to 1968. The right-hander won 24 for the Cubs in 1964. Lifetime record: 194–183.

Bob Buhl, a hard thrower and a winner for the Braves through most of the 1950s. He also worked for the Cubs and Phillies. For his 15-year National League career Bob was 166–132.

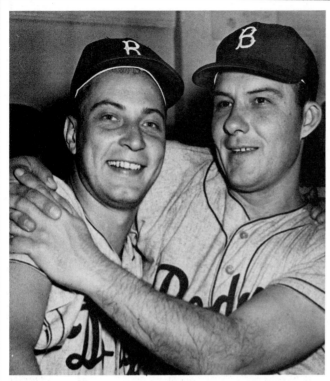

Johnny Podres (left) and catcher Rube Walker celebrating a Podres shutout of the Giants in September 1957. Johnny, a gifted southpaw, pitched for the Dodgers from 1953 to 1966. His career mark is 148–116.

Jim Brosnan, right-hander with the Cubs, Cardinals, and Reds from 1954 to 1963. He authored several first-rate books dealing with his baseball experiences.

Busch Stadium in St. Louis, home of the Cardinals and site of the 1957 All-Star Game, when this photo was taken.

Most Valuable Player Ernie Banks receiving his plaque from National League President Warren Giles in 1959.

Orlando Cepeda. He had a fine career in the National League with the Giants, Cardinals, and Braves from 1958 to 1972, batting over .300 nine times. He was MVP with the Cardinals in 1967. Lifetime average: .297, with 379 home runs.

Jim Davenport, slick-fielding third baseman for the Giants from 1958 to 1970.

Ebbets Field, abandoned by the Dodgers in 1957 when they headed west.

Sam Jones, a right-hander with a world of stuff. He pitched for the Cubs, Cardinals, and Giants, winning 21 for San Francisco in 1959. Overall he was 102–101.

Wally Moon, smooth-stroking outfielder with the Cardinals and Dodgers from 1954 to 1965. Career average: .289.

Dick Stuart, colorful first baseman with the Pirates from 1958 to 1962. Dick always swung for the fences, and over his career, which lasted until 1969, hit 228 home runs.

Danny Murtaugh consoling Harvey Haddix after the Pittsburgh lefty lost his historic 12-inning perfect game to Milwaukee in the thirteenth inning on May 26, 1959.

Bill Mazeroski, hero of the 1960 World Series for the Pirates, played second base for Pittsburgh from 1956 to 1972 and set the standard. Bill batted .260 lifetime.

Dick Groat, top-ranked shortstop in the National League from 1952 to 1967. Dick's .325 batting average led the league in 1960, the year he was the league's MVP for the Pirates. He batted .286 lifetime.

Roberto Clemente is out at home, neatly blocked by the Giants' Hobie Landrith. The action took place in May 1960.

Pittsburgh's ace in the 1960 pennant year, right-hander Vernon Law. He was 20–9, winning the Cy Young Award. Law pitched for the Pirates from 1950 to 1967, winning 162 and losing 147.

Sandy Koufax. Lifetime record: 165–87. Over his last five seasons, 1962 to 1966, he was 111–34.

8

From Koufax to Seaver

It began coming together for the Brooklyn-born Koufax in 1961. Joining the Dodgers as a bonus player in 1955, the hard-throwing lefty had had to serve his apprenticeship in the big leagues because of then-existing rules applying to players who received a sizable bonus. Unable to pitch regularly because he was on a club that generally was in contention, and plagued by wildness when he did get a chance to go to the mound, Koufax's development was slow and arduous. Aflame with competitive zeal and motivated by gritty determination, the quiet, modest, intelligent young man kept working. He realized that he would not be a winner until he achieved control, and that control in the big leagues meant more than just getting the ball over the plate; it meant putting it in spots, pitching to a hitter's weakness.

To some fans it may have seemed like an overnight miracle, but to Koufax it was the payoff of a half dozen years of hard work. In 1961 he arrived at the brink of all-time greatness with an 18–13 record and a league-leading 269 strikeouts in 256 innings. Taking his regular turn now along with fellow starters Johnny Podres, Don Drysdale, and Stan Williams, Sandy walked just 96 men in his 256 innings, an indication that the most awesome pitching talent since Bob Feller was ready to explode on the baseball scene.

Expansion became a reality in 1961, with the American League going to ten teams. It was the last year of the eight-team National League and it saw Fred Hutchinson's Cincinnati Reds end a 21-year drought with a 4-game pennant victory over the Dodgers. The Reds had a 21-game winner in righty Joey Jay, acquired from the Braves over the winter, and a 19-gamer in lefty Jim O'Toole.

They also packed a potent one-two punch in outfielders Frank Robinson and Vada Pinson, who batted .323 and .343 respectively. The league's top hitter, though, was Pittsburgh's Roberto Clemente, who took the first of his four batting titles, with a .351 average.

The year was highlighted by some scintillating achievements as well as one particularly dismal one. On April 28, the ageless Warren Spahn hurled the second no-hitter of his distinguished career, baffling a lineup that included heavy gunners like Willie Mays, Orlando Cepeda, Harvey Kuenn, and Felipe Alou. Two days later, in the same series at Milwaukee, Mays had the greatest day of his career, when he shot four home runs out of County Stadium. On August 11 the forty-year-old Spahn, on the way to his twelfth 20-game season, became only the third National League pitcher in the twentieth century, after Mathewson and Alexander, to win 300 games, when he edged the Cubs 2–1. The season's low point was struck by the Phillies between July 29 and August 20, when they lost 23 games in a row, most by any big-league team in the twentieth century.

The National League expanded to ten teams in 1962, establishing outposts in Houston and New York. The team that brought National League ball back to the big city immediately became the most colorful and lovable losers in baseball, managed by one of baseball's most colorful and lovable winners—Casey Stengel. Stengel, dropped by the Yankees two years before for the sin of becoming seventy years old (which the old man said he would never make the mistake of doing again), saw his Mets lose 120 games of the league's new expanded 162-game schedule, making them the most prolific losers in history.

There was another, more positive, record set in 1962 and it proved to be a watershed performance in modern baseball history. Ty Cobb's 1915 record of 96 stolen bases long had been thought out of reach. If for many years there had been a dead ball, when few

home runs were hit, similarly there seemed to be a "dead base path," when comparatively few bases were stolen. For years, National League-leading base-stealers were counting their thefts in the thirties, with Willie Mays' 40 in 1956 the highest total since 1929.

In 1961 Dodger shortstop Maury Wills pumped some new life into the moribund art form of legal thievery when he swiped 50 bags, best in the league since Max Carey's 51 in 1923. Maury's performance was a good one; but it hardly prepared anyone for what he achieved the following season. Running with speed and calculation, the slender, wing-footed Wills stole an astounding 104 bases, smashing Cobb's 47-year-old record and opening a new era in baseball.

Knocking Maury around the bases he did not steal was teammate Tommy Davis, who took titles with a .346 batting average and 153 runs batted in. Also having his greatest year was right-hander Don Drysdale with a 25–9 record. Behind these sterling efforts, the best the Dodgers could do was manage a first-place tie with the Giants, and if not for a midseason ailment that befell Koufax, the Dodgers would no doubt have had first place to themselves at the close of the regular season.

Koufax was on his way to a blazing season when he came down with a mysterious circulatory ailment in the fingers of his pitching hand. Riding a 14–5 record at the time, heading for a new major-league strikeout record, Sandy was all but lost for the final three months of the season. He did put in enough work, however, to capture the first of five consecutive earned-run-average crowns.

The Giants, led by Jack Sanford's 24 wins and the thundering bats of Mays, Cepeda, Willie McCovey, and Felipe Alou, who accounted for 129 of the team's 204 home runs, fought the Dodgers to a tie and set the stage for the National League's fourth pennant play-off, all four of which featured the Dodgers.

It was 1951 all over again for the Dodgers. After splitting the first two games, the

Dodgers took a 4–2 lead into the top of the ninth inning of the decisive third game, only to see the Giants erupt for four runs and the snatching away of another flag.

The year was also a personal triumph for forty-one-year-old Stan Musial. Challenging for the batting title throughout most of the summer, the venerable slugger ended with a .330 mark, his last big year. And on May 19 Stan's single off of Los Angeles lefty Ron Perranoski put him on top of the heap as the league's all-time hit collector. It was number 3,431 and dropped Honus Wagner into second place.

As they had done in 1952, the Dodgers bounced back from eleventh-hour heartbreak to take the pennant the next year. This time they had the peerless Koufax for the full span, and Sandy showed the world just how good he really was. The fireballer spun out a dazzling 25–5 season, led in ERA with 1.88, strikeouts with 306, and shutouts with 11. What Sandy couldn't finish, Ron Perranoski did. The relief pitcher logged a 16–3 record with 21 saves.

Koufax's superb year overshadowed one almost equally as good by the Giants' right-hander Juan Marichal. The Dominican mound artist was 25–8. Year after year Marichal put together comparable seasons, but always in the shadow of the mighty Koufax. It was like being a home run hitter in the days of Ruth or a high-average man in the days of Hornsby. The light at the very top was just too blinding.

Also overshadowed were 23–7 years by Cincinnati's own blazing-fast Jim Maloney and Milwaukee's Warren Spahn. For the forty-two-year-old Spahn it was his thirteenth and last 20-game season.

The 1963 season also closed out the career of Stan Musial. The Man called it quits after batting .255. He left behind a National League record 3,630 hits. It seemed a record that would stand for a long, long time. Actually, it stood for 18 years. When Musial collected his final hit, on September 29 against

Cincinnati, watching the ball sail into the outfield was a rookie second baseman named Pete Rose. The switch-hitting youngster, who in time would make his own determined, relentless assault on the record book, batted .273 and was voted Rookie of the Year.

In 1950, a Philadelphia Phillies team dissipated a seven-game lead in the last nine games of the season and barely squeaked through to win the pennant, thanks to the strong right arm of Robin Roberts. Fourteen years later, in 1964, another Philadelphia Phillies team came charging down the stretch with an ostensibly insurmountable lead. Again the team faltered, and this time there was no Robin Roberts to call upon. Beginning on September 20, Gene Mauch's club lost ten straight games, while the Cardinals launched a late-season drive that saw them take eight in a row and the pennant by one game over the stunned Phillies, who ended up tying Cincinnati for second place.

It was a very solid Cardinal team that won this pennant. Although left-handed Ray Sadecki won 20 games, the ace was a twenty-eight-year-old righty who threw as hard as anybody in the league. His name was Bob Gibson. Gibson, a fine all-around athlete who could field and run and hit as well as strike people out, was as hard-nosed a competitor as ever took the mound. The flame that burned under his pride and zeal to excel remained hot and inextinguishable throughout a 17-year career that climaxed with his election to the Hall of Fame.

The Cardinal hitting was done by first baseman Bill White, ex-Pittsburgh shortstop Dick Groat, third baseman Ken Boyer, catcher Tim McCarver, and outfielders Curt Flood and Lou Brock. The twenty-five-year-old Brock had been obtained in a midseason swap with the Cubs for pitcher Ernie Broglio. Broglio, who had had some fine seasons for the Cardinals, never panned out for the Cubs, winning but seven games for them as he struggled through three seasons. Brock, on the other hand, rose to all-time base-stealing heights, becoming the catalyst of the St. Louis attack and one of the most exciting players of his era.

The game of the year was hurled by Jim Bunning, ace of the ill-fated Phillies. On June 21 the tall right-hander fired a perfect game against Casey Stengel's hapless Mets. It was the first perfect-game victory in the National League in the twentieth century. It was also the second memorable exercise in futility for the Mets in a month. On May 31 a crowd of 57,000 jammed brand-new Shea Stadium in New York to watch a doubleheader between their heroes and the San Francisco Giants. The Giants took the first game by a score of 5–3. The second game, however, went 23 innings before the Giants finally took it, 8–6. Playing time for the doubleheader was eight minutes short of ten hours, a record for diamond entertainment.

Some high-class pitching by Koufax and Drysdale brought the Dodgers back to the top of the heap in 1965. Sandy was 26–8 with a major-league record 382 strikeouts, a fourth consecutive ERA title, and for good luck a perfect game against the Cubs on September 9. Sandy won it by a 1–0 score as Chicago lefty Bob Hendley pitched a losing one-hitter. Almost matching Koufax win for win all season long was Don Drysdale with a 23–12 record. Between them, the two aces struck out nearly 600 batters.

With an attack that was strictly popgun, the Dodgers needed golden arms on the mound to win. Maury Wills was the team's most potent threat, and Maury did it with his legs, stealing 94 bases to lead in that department for the sixth-straight time.

The pennant race boiled down to another Dodger-Giant run for the wire, with each team turning on the heat in September, the Dodgers with a 13-game win streak, the Giants with a stretch of 14 in a row. At the end it was Walter Alston's boys by two lengths. Despite the Giants' disappointment at the end, it was a year of personal triumph for Willie Mays, who hit 52 home runs. In Cincinnati the twenty-four-year-old Peter Edward Rose put on a year-long display of two new habits he had acquired: he batted .300 for the first time and he led the league with 209 hits. In time Pete Rose's .300 batting average and 200 hits became the most predictable and exciting ritual of the National League summer.

The 1966 season found the Braves playing in a brand-new National League city, Atlanta. The Braves' honeymoon in Milwaukee had lasted just 13 years. As the team's fortunes declined, so did attendance. Actually, the club had hoped to head south in 1965, but with a year remaining on their stadium lease they were compelled to stay hunkered down in Milwaukee for the 1965 season. The disenchanted fans virtually ignored the lame-duck team and attendance was a meager 555,584.

With Atlanta fans now cheering Henry Aaron and his 40-home-run bat, the club's attendance nearly tripled despite a fifth-place finish. At the top of the league there was another nail-biter. It was the Dodgers again, behind their strong pitching, squeaking through to finish 1½ games up on the Giants and three ahead of a Pittsburgh club that featured a bruising offense but little front-line pitching.

The great Koufax reached new heights this year, winning 27 and losing 9, taking a fifth-straight ERA title with a breathtaking 1.73 mark for 323 innings. Behind the matchless lefty were Drysdale, Claude Osteen, rookie Don Sutton, and bullpen operatives Perranoski and Phil Regan, who had a 14–1 record.

For the Giants, Marichal's superb 25–6 season was again overshadowed by the left-hander down the coast, as was a strong 21–8 effort by righty Gaylord Perry. Pittsburgh's heavy hitting was done mainly by power man Willie Stargell, batting champion Matty Alou (.342), Donn Clendenon, Manny Mota, and MVP Roberto Clemente.

In 1966 the league as a whole batted .249; a year later the collective average was .256.

Part of the rise could be attributed to the retirement at the age of thirty of Koufax. All year long in 1966 the southpaw had been pitching in pain due to an arthritic left elbow. After each game he was forced to soak the priceless arm in ice for half an hour. Warned by doctors that continued abuse of the arm could cause serious and lasting damage, Koufax announced his retirement, bringing to a close one of the most glittering pitching careers in all of baseball. Over his last five seasons the Dodger ace had compiled an 111–34 won-lost record—as close to unbeatable as major-league pitchers come.

Without Koufax, the Dodgers had little chance of taking a third-straight flag, and indeed sank to eighth place. Taking the pennant in 1967 and again in 1968 were the St. Louis Cardinals, led by the man who had become one of the league's dominant pitchers, Bob Gibson. Held to a 13–7 season in 1967 because of a midseason broken leg, when he was hit by a line shot off the bat of Clemente, Gibson roared back a year later with one of the most astounding seasons in modern times. Bullet Bob blazed to a 22–9 season and a microscopic 1.12 earned-run average, lowest in league history. How Gibson managed to lose nine games with that ERA is perhaps best left to his hitters to explain.

The 1968 season is remembered as "the Year of the Pitcher," the moundsmen holding the hitters to a feeble .243 average. It was the season in which the Dodgers' Don Drysdale hurled six consecutive shutouts and 58⅔ scoreless innings, topping Walter Johnson's 55-year-old record of 56. Overall, 185 shutouts were pitched in 1968, most ever in the league, with Gibson leading with 13. San Francisco's Marichal put together another great season with a 26–9 showing, but this time the Giant righty was fated to be overshadowed by Gibson. Despite a career of almost unparalleled brilliance, Marichal never won a Cy Young Award as his league's premier pitcher.

Alarmed that their game was losing some of its excitement due to pitching dominance, the baseball establishment decreed that in 1969 the pitching mound be lowered six inches and the strike zone tightened up a bit to provide more equity.

It was the year that the league expanded to 12 teams, setting up shop in Montreal and San Diego. Finding a 12-team league too unwieldy, they divided it into a western division and an eastern division with the pennant to be decided by a play-off between the division winners. The West consisted of San Francisco, Los Angeles, Cincinnati, Houston, San Diego, and, by some geographical magic, Atlanta. The East consisted of New York, Chicago, Pittsburgh, St. Louis, Montreal, and Philadelphia.

Batting averages improved only slightly in the pitcher-strong league. What the changes did produce, however, was one pure, unadulterated, and utterly enchanting miracle.

Since their inception in 1962, the New York Mets had never finished higher than ninth and there was no reason to suppose they would do any better in 1969. But they did. Much. With ex-Brooklyn slugger Gil Hodges at the helm, the team had assembled a cast of strong young pitchers. At the top of the staff was a handsome, twenty-four-year-old right-hander named Tom Seaver. The intelligent, articulate, charismatic pitcher had literally been picked out of a hat by the Mets. Originally signed by the Braves, his contract was voided by the league because of a violation of a technicality in organized baseball's agreement with colleges that stipulated a player could not be signed until his class had graduated. Seaver's class at USC had not graduated when he signed his $50,000 bonus contract; therefore he was declared a free agent. The commissioner told the teams that were interested in signing the young man to put their names into a hat and one would be drawn out. About a half dozen clubs participated in the drawing. The paper that was lifted from the hat had New York Mets written on it. Seaver accepted the Mets' offer.

Joining the Mets in 1967 after one year in the minors, Tom won 16 games in each of his first two years. In 1969 he blossomed into the league's top pitcher, winning 25 and losing 7. Behind him was left-hander Jerry Koosman with a 17–9 record. Also on the staff was a twenty-two-year-old fireballer with an arm so live it probably vibrated while he slept. His name was Nolan Ryan. In the bullpen was lefty Tug McGraw, winning 9 and saving 12.

With Seaver and Koosman winning their last 19 games in August and September, the Mets, without a true star in their lineup, barreled through the stunned league and won the eastern division title with 100 victories. They came in eight lengths ahead of Leo Durocher's Cubs, who outhit and outscored them in every category and who had a pair of 20-gamers in Ferguson Jenkins and Bill Hands. The Mets were in fact outscored by eight teams in the league. Tommie Agee's 75 runs batted in were tops on the club. Twenty-three men in the league knocked in more than the Mets' top gun, but it didn't matter, for this was a team of destiny.

The Atlanta Braves won the first western division title, thanks to 44 big ones by Henry Aaron and 23 wins by knuckle baller Phil Niekro. But the Braves fell in three straight in the league's first championship series. Typically, when their pitching failed, the Mets turned around and outslugged the Braves in each game. Probably the archetypical Mets game was played in St. Louis on the night of September 15. Steve Carlton, the Cardinals' hard-throwing left-hander, set a new record by fanning 19 batters, only to lose 4–3 on a pair of two-run homers by the Mets' Ron Swoboda.

There were no miracles the next year. The Mets finished third, six games behind a Pittsburgh team led by Clemente's .353 batting average. The high point of the 1970 season for the Mets came on April 22 at Shea Stadium, when Seaver tied Carlton's record by striking out 19 San Diego batters in one game, including the last ten in a row.

In the western division it was Cincinnati, under freshman skipper Sparky Anderson. It was a club getting set to dominate most of the decade of the 1970s. Winning 102 games and finishing 14½ ahead of the Dodgers, the Reds' attack featured .300 hitters Tony Perez, Pete Rose, Bobby Tolan, and Bernie Carbo. The biggest gun on the club was its twenty-two-year-old catcher, Johnny Bench, who hit 45 home runs and drove in 148 runs to become the league's hardest-hitting catcher since Roy Campanella.

"To Johnny Bench, a future Hall of Famer," wrote a prescient Ted Williams in autographing a ball to the youngster. Perhaps the greatest catcher in National League history, Bench was born with an abundance of baseball skills. Not only was he blessed with great power and a cannonlike throwing arm, but he brought to catching instincts and knowledge that had to be wholly innate.

Though the championship series between Pittsburgh and Cincinnati in 1970 was closely played—the scores were 3–0, 3–1, 3–2,—it all went Cincinnati's way. They were not "the Big Red Machine" quite yet, but they were gearing up. With a few shrewd trades and a fertile farm system, they would become in a few years perhaps the finest team ever to play in the National League.

Right-hander Joey Jay, 21-game winner with Cincinnati in 1961 and 1962. Lifetime he was 99–91.

Vada Pinson, Cincinnati outfielder from 1958 to 1968, and an 18-year major leaguer overall. Lifetime average: .286.

Righty Bob Purkey worked for the Pirates, Reds, and Cardinals from 1954 to 1966. His big year was 1962, when he was 23–5 for the Reds. Over his career he was 129–115.

Willie Mays unloading one of the four home runs he hit against the Braves in Milwaukee on April 30, 1961.

Felipe Alou, oldest of the three Alou brothers, each of whom came up with the San Francisco Giants.

The great Juan Marichal, Giant ace from 1960 to 1973. Six times a 20-game winner, his lifetime r
243–142.

Jesus Alou.

Matty Alou, the youngest brother. A lifetime .307 hitter and the 1966 batting champion with a .342 average for Pittsburgh.

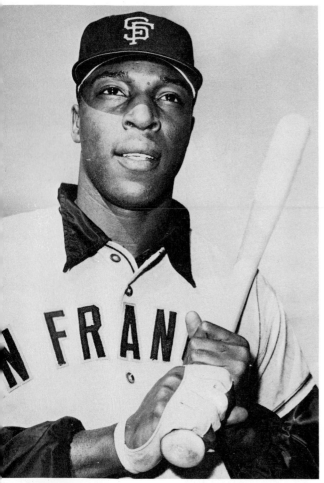

Willie McCovey, from 1959 to 1980 one of the National League's most feared hitters. Three times the home run leader, Willie hit 521 four-baggers and batted .270.

Right-hander Jack Sanford, 19–8 as a Phillie rookie in 1957 and 24–7 with the Giants in 1962. Lifetime he stands at 137–101.

George Altman, outfielder who had some solid seasons for the Cubs in the early 1960s.

Leo ("Chico") Cardenas, Cincinnati's fine shortstop from 1960 to 1968.

Roberto Clemente climbing the fence in San Francisco in a futile attempt to take Hobie Landrith's home run. The action occurred in April 1961.

Chris Short, hard-throwing Phillie left-hander in the 1960s. Chris was 20–10 for the Phillies in 1966 and 135–132 lifetime.

Walter Alston.

Maury Wills. His 104 stolen bases in 1962 remains a landmark achievement.

Tommy Davis, a hitter with a natural line-drive stroke. Tommy was the National League's batting champion in 1962 and 1963. He broke in with the Dodgers in 1959 and played for ten clubs in an 18-year major-league career. Lifetime average: .294.

Don Drysdale, top-rank Dodger right-hander from 1956 to 1969, during which time he compiled a 209–166 record.

Sandy Koufax in full stride.

Warren Spahn, one of the National League's consummate mound artists. With a career record of 363–245, he is second only to Mathewson and Alexander in total wins in league history.

Nobody could throw harder than Jim Maloney, Cincinnati pitcher from 1960 to 1970. Jim was 23–7 in 1963, 134–84 overall.

Pete Rose in 1964.

Rusty Staub in 1966.

Relief pitcher Ron Perranoski had his best years with the Dodgers in the 1960s. Ron appeared in 737 games in his career, all but 736 as a starter.

The infamous Marichal-Roseboro incident on August 22, 1965. Marichal thought the Dodger catcher was making his return throws a bit too close to Marichal's head and suddenly turned and attacked him with the bat. Sandy Koufax has run in to help break it up.

Ken Boyer, stellar third baseman from 1955 to 1969, most of those years spent with the Cardinals. He was National League MVP in 1964. He drove in 90 or more runs eight times and had a career batting average of .287.

Bill White, heavy-hitting first baseman with the Giants, Cardinals, and Phillies from 1956 to 1969. Lifetime average: .286.

Joe Torre, good-hitting catcher and first baseman with the Braves, Cardinals, and Mets (whom he later managed) from 1960 to 1977. Joe led in batting in 1971 with a .363 average and was voted MVP in the National League. He hit .297 lifetime.

Jim Bunning pitched in the big leagues for 17 years, including his last eight (1964 to 1971) for the Phillies, Pirates, and Dodgers. Overall he was 224–184.

Curt Flood, the Cardinals' gifted center fielder from 1958 to 1969. Curt hit
over .300 six times and .293 lifetime.

Gaylord Perry.

Jim Ray Hart, long-ball-hitting third baseman for the Giants in the 1960s.

Bob Veale, talented and hard-throwing Pittsburgh left-hander in the 1960s. Lifetime record: 120–95.

Claude Osteen, one of the mainstays of the fine Dodger pitching staffs from 1965 to 1973. A big leaguer from 1957 to 1975, his career record is 196–195.

Jimmy Wynn, long baller for the Astros and Dodgers.

Gifted and controversial, Richie Allen was one of the premier big guns of his era, 1963 to 1977. He hit 40 home runs for the Phillies in 1966. Lifetime average: .292.

Larry Dierker, 20-game winner for Houston in 1969.

Lou Brock.

Lou Brock stealing a base against Cincinnati in September 1966. The young second baseman is Pete Rose.

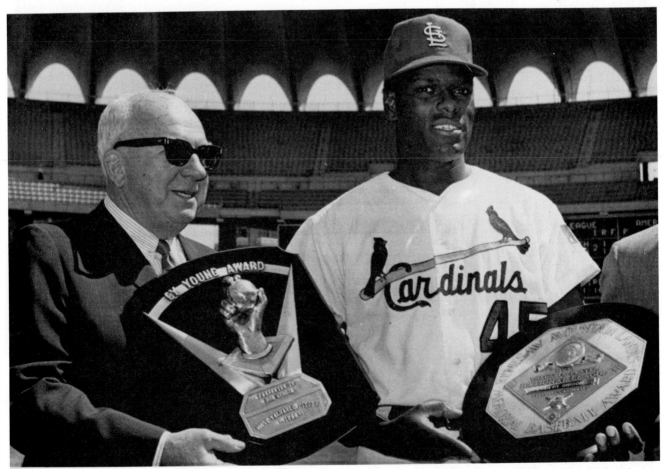

Warren Giles making another presentation. This time it is the Cy Young Award and Most Valuable Player Award, both of which the Cardinals' Bob Gibson won in 1968.

Ferguson Jenkins.

Ron Santo, Cub third baseman from 1960 to 1973 and one of the best. He had 342 home runs and a .277 lifetime average.

Steve Carlton (left) and his favorite catcher, Tim McCarver.

Willie Mays.

Shortstop Don Kessinger.

Second baseman Glenn Beckert.

The Chicago Cubs' crack double-play combination
in the 1960s.

Ken Holtzman. Lifetime record: 168–141.

The Cubs' Billy Williams, one of the toughest hitters in the National League from 1959 to 1974. From September 1963 through September 1970, he played in 1,117 consecutive games, setting a National League record.

Tom Seaver.

A full house at New York's Shea Stadium, home of the Mets.

The Mets' Jerry Grote, one of the fine defensive catchers of his era.

Bobby Bonds.

Some key cogs in Cincinnati's "Big Red Machine." With Johnny Bench in the driver's seat, the others are (left to right) Bobby Tolan, Tony Perez, Lee May, and Pete Rose.

Jerry Koosman.

Outfielder Tommie Agee of the 1969 Mets.

Rico Carty, National League batting champion with Atlanta in 1970 with a .366 average.

Steve Blass, ace Pittsburgh right-hander. Lifetime record: 103–76.

Dave Giusti, king of the Pirate bullpen in the 1970s.

Roberto Clemente.

Johnny Bench.

9

In the Money

The Reds stumbled in 1971 and finished fourth in the six-team western division. An off-season injury suffered by Bobby Tolan kept the gifted outfielder out of action for the entire year, while neither Tony Perez nor Johnny Bench was able to come close to repeating his banner 1970 season. The most significant thing to happen to the Reds was a little-noticed early-season swap they made with San Francisco: Cincinnati sent shortstop Frank Duffy and a minor-league pitcher to the Giants for a young outfielder named George Foster.

Despite their propensity for disastrous trades—in less than a decade they had traded, with little to show for it, the three Alou brothers, Orlando Cepeda, and now Foster—the Giants battled to the division title, edging Alston's Dodgers by a single game. With McCovey losing a lot of time to injuries and Mays beginning to give ground to the years, the Giants were picked up by a fine year by right fielder Bobby Bonds, who clouted 33 home runs.

In the East it was the Pirates again, with a lineup of big busters led by Willie Stargell, whose 48 homers edged out Henry Aaron's 47 for the league lead. On April 27 Aaron whiplashed home run number 600, joining Babe Ruth and Mays as the only men ever to hit over 600 four-baggers. Along with Stargell, the Pirates had young first baseman Bob Robertson with 26 home runs, a .341 season from Clemente, and fine showings by Al Oliver, Dave Cash, and Manny Sanguillen, a .319-hitting catcher who liked to swing the bat—in over 550 appearances Manny drew just 19 walks.

Chicago Cubs right-hander Ferguson Jenkins, a tall, hard thrower with superb control, was 24–13, a 20-game winner for the fifth consecutive season.

One of the few beneficial trade acquisitions the team had made in recent times, Jenkins had been obtained from the Phillies in 1966 and promptly began launching seasons of high winning. In 1971 the Cub ace walked just 37 men in 325 innings, an exhibition of control reminiscent of the days of Christy Mathewson and Grover Cleveland Alexander.

In the 1971 championship series it was Pittsburgh over the Giants in four games, with Bob Robertson putting on a power display for the Pirates in the second game with three home runs.

Pittsburgh made it three eastern division titles in a row in 1972, easily outdistancing the second-place Cubs by 11 games, despite a sixth consecutive 20-game season by Jenkins. The Pirates enjoyed fine pitching all summer long by righties Steve Blass, Dock Ellis, Nelson Briles, and relief ace Dave Giusti to go along with the usual heavy stickwork from Stargell, Clemente, Oliver, Cash, and Richie Hebner.

In the West it was all Cincinnati. The Reds had acquired second baseman Joe Morgan from Houston in a trade that sent their home run-hitting first baseman Lee May to the Astros. Bench had a big comeback season with 40 homers and 125 runs batted in, both league-leading numbers. Despite a pitching staff that had 15-game winner Gary Nolan as its biggest winner, Sparky Anderson manipulated shrewdly all season, thanks to a deep bullpen that included right-handers Clay Carroll and Pedro Borbon and lefty Tom Hall. Sparky's staff turned in just 25 complete games, lowest in the league. Anderson's quick, decisive trips to the mound soon earned him the nickname "Captain Hook," an appellation his starters did not always use with a smile.

The championship series went five games, with Pittsburgh losing on a heartbreaking note in the bottom of the ninth of the fifth game. Ahead 3–2, the Pirates saw the Reds tie the score on a towering home run by Bench, and

then win it a few moments later when Bob Moose wild-pitched home the winning run.

The most remarkable performance of the year was turned in by Philadelphia left-hander Steve Carlton. Piqued by Carlton's salary demands, the Cardinals had traded their 20-game winner to the Phillies for pitcher Rick Wise, a steady but not spectacular winner. Pitching with relentless fury all season long, Carlton hung up a 27–10 record for a last-place team that won just 59 games. The big lefty had an ERA of 1.98, fanned 310 batters, and completed 30 of 41 starts as he became the biggest drawing card in Philadelphia baseball history and the league's most formidable southpaw since Koufax.

For the thirty-seven-year-old Roberto Clemente it was another routine season. The Pirate right fielder, though slowed by an ankle injury, batted .312. In the last game of the season Clemente collected his three thousandth major-league hit. It was to be the last of his illustrious career. On December 31 Clemente and several others set off from San Juan, Puerto Rico, in a shaky DC-7 to fly provisions to earthquake victims in Nicaragua. Almost as soon as it was airborne, the plane plummeted into the sea, taking with it Clemente and his companions.

In 1973 the New York Mets rose to the top of the eastern division once more despite barely playing .500 ball, ending with an 82–79 record. The Mets emerged from a tight race on a September splurge, goaded by relief ace Tug McGraw's "Ya gotta believe!" rallying cry. When the final bell rang, the Cardinals were 1½ games behind, the Pirates 2½, and Montreal 3½, each club in contention until the final weekend.

Again it was pitching that buoyed the Mets, Seaver winning 19, and lefties Jerry Koosman and Jon Matlack 14 apiece, while lefty George Stone sparkled with a 12–3 mark. McGraw was tremendous coming down the stretch, ending with 25 saves. The Mets' team batting average of .246 placed them ninth in the 12-

team league and they were outscored by every club except one—an amazing statistic.

Keeping Montreal in the race until the end was iron-man relief pitcher Mike Marshall, a flinty individualist with unorthodox theories about kinesthesia, the sensation of movement or strain in muscles, tendons, and joints. Mike proved it made sense by appearing in a record 92 games, winning 14 and saving 31, giving him a hand (or an arm) in 45 of Montreal's 79 victories.

For Atlanta's Henry Aaron the season ended on a drawn breath that would have to be held until 1974. The Braves' slugger pounded 40 home runs to draw to within one of Babe Ruth's all-time record 714. Slamming away right alongside Henry all season long in the Atlanta launching pad were third baseman Darrell Evans with 41 homers and second baseman Dave Johnson with 43. It was the first time any club ever had three 40-homer men in one season, with Johnson's 43 a record for second basemen.

In the West it was Cincinnati outlegging the Dodgers by 3½ lengths. The Big Red Machine was gearing up now. Tony Perez batted .314 with 27 home runs; Joe Morgan batted .290 with 26 home runs; shortstop Dave Concepcion batted .287; Pete Rose batted .338 to lead the league and collected 230 hits, also a top figure; while Johnny Bench connected for 25 home runs. On the mound Sparky Anderson had a 19-game winner in Jack Billingham and an 18-game man in young left-hander Don Gullett.

Cincinnati was clearly the best team in the league in 1973; but as baseball men are wont to say, in a short series anything can happen. And anything is exactly what happened in the 1973 championship series. The Mets, with their barely .500 record, upset the Reds in five games, thanks to some hearty pitching by Seaver, Koosman, and Matlack.

The big event of 1974 was the inevitable happening—Henry Aaron's record-breaking home run. With the schedule placing the

Braves in Cincinnati for their first three games, Braves' President Bill Bartholomay ordered Aaron to sit out the first three games in the hope that Henry's quest for Ruth's record would sell out the park in Atlanta. This blatant exploitation was overriden by Commissioner Bowie Kuhn, who ruled it would be inequitable to sit Aaron down for this reason.

So Aaron opened the season in Cincinnati and wasted no time, sending out home run number 714 on his first at bat. Four days later, at home in Atlanta, Aaron crashed number 715 off of Los Angeles lefty Al Downing to establish a new all-time home run record.

There was another record-making performance in 1974, not as dramatic as Aaron's, but highly impressive nevertheless. Whereas Ty Cobb's single-season stolen base record had stood for 47 years until broken by Maury Wills in 1962, Wills' record lasted for just 12 years. St. Louis' Lou Brock smashed Maury's standard of 104 with plenty to spare, the Cardinal whippet stealing successfully 118 times. It was no freak season. Lou had been gearing for it, having led the league in seven of the previous eight seasons. To show how far the art of the stolen base had progressed, Brock's total was exactly 100 better than the leader in 1941, Philadelphia second baseman Danny Murtaugh, now managing the Pirates.

There was still another record-making performance in 1974, this one by reliever Mike Marshall, now working for the Dodgers. Marshall broke his own record by going to the mound 106 times. "He told me he could do it," Dodger Manager Walter Alston said with a shrug. "And I let him."

In spite of Brock's 118 stolen bases and some good hitting by outfielder Reggie Smith and young catcher Ted Simmons, Murtaugh's Pirates slipped in by 1½ games to take the eastern division title for the fourth time in five years. With Jerry Reuss topping the staff with just 16 victories, the Pirates once again did it with muscle, most of it supplied by Richie Hebner, Richie Zisk, Willie Stargell, and Al

Oliver.

Led by the tireless Mike Marshall and 20-game winner Andy Messersmith, the Dodgers took the western division title by four games over the Reds. The Los Angeles club had put together a young infield of Steve Garvey at first, Davey Lopes at second, Bill Russell at shortstop, and Ron Cey at third. This quartet was going to establish a record for togetherness by remaining intact through the 1981 season.

In the championship series the Dodgers, with Don Sutton hurling two strong games in which he held the powerful Pirates to just seven hits, won the pennant in four games.

The Big Red Machine rolled irresistibly during 1975 and 1976, winning 108 and 102 games, swamping the Dodgers by 20 games in 1975 and by 10 a year later. Sparky Anderson's club was perhaps the greatest ever put together in the National League, with the possible exception of some of the Brooklyn Dodger teams in the 1950s.

Stability was one of the key features of this team. It was the same eight regulars in each of the two pennant years: Perez, Morgan, Concepcion, and Rose in the infield; Ken Griffey, Cesar Geronimo, and George Foster in the outfield; Johnny Bench behind the plate. All of them played full seasons. Morgan was the MVP in each year. In 1975 when the club won 108 games, third highest ever in the league and the best since Pittsburgh's 110 in 1909, not one of Anderson's pitchers won more than 15. Sparky had six winners in double figures, led by 15-gamers Don Gullett, Gary Nolan, and Jack Billingham. Again Anderson manipulated a deep bullpen that included veterans Pedro Borbon and Clay Carroll and youngsters Rawly Eastwick and Will McEnaney.

The 1976 club, again with a 15-game winner (Nolan) at the top of the staff, was a totally dominant outfit, with five .300 hitters. The club led the league in every offensive category known to statisticians, and led in fielding percentage and fewest errors as well. They were awesome and utterly unbeatable.

In 1975 the Pirates won the eastern division title for the fifth time in six years, only to be rolled under in three straight by the Reds. In 1976 a strong Philadelphia team, led by home run champion Mike Schmidt, Greg Luzinski, Garry Maddox, and 20-game winner Steve Carlton, also bowed in three straight to the Reds.

Toward the end of 1975 a decision was handed down by baseball arbitrator Peter Seitz that was destined to send the game into the era of free agency, the reentry draft, and skyrocketing salaries. Two pitchers, the Dodgers' Andy Messersmith and Montreal's Dave McNally, had elected to play the 1975 season without signing their contracts. The club owners invoked the reserve clause in the players' previously signed contracts. This clause provided that a player remained bound to the club holding his contract whether he signs for another year or not. The players maintained that playing out their option years without signing a contract entitled them to free agency at the conclusion of the season and the right to sell themselves to the highest bidders. The question was submitted to arbitration.

On December 23, 1975, Seitz announced his decision: a player who "plays out" his contract by not signing for a year has discharged his contractual obligations. Messersmith and McNally were therefore free to sign with whomever they wished. McNally, who had been lending his name to the test case, retired after the season, but Messersmith negotiated a lucrative seven-figure contract with Atlanta.

The Seitz decision led to some bitter wrangling between the players and the owners, the players claiming there was now no longer any such thing as a reserve clause, while the owners insisted the decision applied only to the two men involved. The owners petitioned the courts to overturn the decision, without success.

In the summer of 1976 the Players Association and the owners agreed upon a new modified version of the reserve system: any player who wished could become a free agent after six years in the major leagues. However, those who became free agents would not be completely free; a reentry draft would be held after each season and a free agent could only negotiate with a maximum of 13 clubs that, in the reentry draft, had acquired the right to bargain with him. Inevitably, this led to bidding wars, and the era of baseball millionaires began.

In 1977 the Dodgers, playing under their first managerial change in 23 years—Walter Alston having retired the previous fall—got off to a fast start and never faltered, taking the western division title by ten games over the Reds. This was in spite of Cincinnati's mid-season acquisition of the Mets' great right-hander Tom Seaver, who had been having a contractual dispute with the Mets management. The Reds' George Foster put together a monumental season with 52 home runs and 149 runs batted in, league-leading figures that earned him the Most Valuable Player Award, the fifth Cincinnati player in six years to be so designated.

Rookie Manager Tom Lasorda's Dodgers employed strong pitching, most notably a 20-game season from lefty Tommy John, and some power hitting—30-homer seasons from Steve Garvey, Ron Cey, Reggie Smith, and Dusty Baker—to break Cincinnati's grip on the West.

In the East it was Philadelphia again, and again it was Steve Carlton (23–10) and home run busters Mike Schmidt and Greg Luzinski, who hit 77 between them, leading the way. The Phillies' attack was steady and solid up and down the lineup, with Schmidt's .274 average the lowest among the regulars.

For the Phillies, however, it was a second-straight postseason disappointment, as they lost the championship series to the Dodgers in four games.

In August of 1977 another hallowed and long-standing record went by the boards when Lou Brock stole the eight hundred ninety-third base of his career, breaking Ty Cobb's all-time record.

Tom Lasorda made it two pennants in two years in 1978, steering the Dodgers in by 2½ games ahead of Cincinnati. As it had been ever since their move to Los Angeles, the Dodger hallmark was pitching, with Lasorda getting plenty of quality hurling from Tommy John, Burt Hooton, Doug Rau, Don Sutton, and Rick Rhoden.

The Phillies made it three straight in the East and almost wished they hadn't, losing a third consecutive championship series. The Philadelphia frustration was heightened this time when, in the tenth inning of the fourth and final game, their sure-handed center fielder, Garry Maddox, dropped an easy chance that led to the winning run.

The Phillies had managed to hold off a late-season charge by Pittsburgh, a club still dominated by their hitters. This year the big Pirate slugger was right fielder Dave Parker, a worthy heir to previous Pittsburgh right fielders Paul Waner and Roberto Clemente. The massive Parker took a second successive batting title, with a .334 average.

The big noise of 1978 in the National League and in all of baseball came from a familiar source. Pete Rose had by now established himself as one of baseball's all-time greats. He was a hitter, a legendary hustler, an inspirational force, a crowd pleaser, an all-star at four different positions, a three-time batting champion. In 1978 he took stage center in a pageant that fit his style, his talent, and his personality with becoming snugness. Beginning on June 14, this American original tore off on a 44-game hitting streak. Before he was finally stopped in Atlanta on August 1, Rose had broken Tommy Holmes' modern National League mark of 37, set in 1945, and tied the pre-1900 record set by Wee Willie Keeler in 1897. Also in this "rosiest" of all his years, Pete achieved another milestone with his three thousandth major-league hit early in May, following Wagner, Paul Waner, Musial, Mays, Aaron, and Clemente into the National League Valhalla (Lou Brock joined this exclusive club a year later).

Rose continued to be big news in the off-season. After being unable to negotiate a new contract with his long-time employers in Cincinnati, the thirty-seven-year-old dynamo declared free agency and eventually signed a multimillion-dollar contract with the Phillies.

Pete gave the Phillies their money's worth in 1979, batting .331 and collecting over 200 hits for the tenth time, breaking yet another long-standing Cobb record. Despite Pete's fine year and 45 home runs from Mike Schmidt, the Phillies finished fourth as Pittsburgh took the title in the East squeezing in two games ahead of a tough young Montreal team.

For the Pirates it was their highly respected, long-time veteran Willie Stargell who paved the way. The thirty-nine-year-old "Pops" popped 32 home runs and shared the MVP Award with St. Louis' batting titlist first baseman Keith Hernandez, who hit .344.

The winningest pitchers in the league turned out to be a pair of knuckle-balling brothers, Atlanta's Phil and Houston's Joe Niekro, each winning 21 games. The league strikeout champ was Houston's awesome 6'8" right-hander J. R. Richard, who rubbed out 313 batters to set a new league record for righties.

In the West, the Reds and Dodgers continued swapping the title around, with Cincinnati coming out on top in 1979, edging Houston by 1½ games. The championship series, however, went to Pittsburgh in three straight. Despite their division title, the Reds were no longer "the Big Red Machine" of previous years. Perez had been traded to Montreal, Rose was with the Phillies, and Morgan had slowed down perceptibly.

The 1980 season saw the Phillies, under hard-driving Dallas Green, regain the top spot in the East. The tough Phillies squad had starring names that were all too familiar to the rest of the league: Pete Rose, Mike Schmidt (48 home runs), and Steve Carlton (24 wins). Again Montreal challenged gamely, hanging on until the regular season's penultimate game, when a Schmidt game-winning homer gave the Phillies the title.

In the western division it was Houston, but not until the Astros had given their fans a severe case of the shakes. Heading into Los Angeles for the season's finale with a three-game lead, Houston lost three tightly played games in a row, setting up a one-game play-off for the division title. Already badly shaken by the loss of ace J. R. Richard to an almost fatal stroke in July, the Astros regrouped and sent 19-game winner Joe Niekro to the mound. Joe made it 20 and Houston left Los Angeles with very little skin on their collective teeth.

The show put on between Philadelphia and Houston for the National League pennant was one of baseball's all-time spectaculars and made the World Series strictly anticlimactic. With four of the games having to go into extra innings for a decision, the Phillies finally took it, three games to two, giving Philadelphia its first pennant in 30 years and only the third in its history.

The 1981 season began sensationally for a twenty-year-old left-handed screwball artist on the staff of the Los Angeles Dodgers. His name was Fernando Valenzuela. The young Mexican had pitched well in a handful of relief appearances coming down the stretch the year before, some of them in pressure situations. He did well in the spring, made the team, and was given the ball on Opening Day, when scheduled starter Jerry Reuss had to be scrubbed because of a leg injury.

Within a month's time Fernando had become a star. By May 14 he was 8–0 with five shutouts. Valenzuela's round, friendly face began appearing on magazine covers all over the country. He was the talk of baseball.

But suddenly there was no more baseball, only talk. On June 12, 1981, major-league ballplayers went out on strike over the issue of compensation being given clubs who lost players to free agency. The Players Association had given clear warning that if the clubs tried to implement this plan, there would be a strike. Accordingly, the clubs did and the players struck.

On June 12 the Phillies were leading the eastern division by 1½ games over the Cardinals, while the Dodgers were heading up the West by half a game over the Reds. By the time the strike was finally settled 52 days later, those slim margins had become highly significant, thanks to some of the most woolly-headed thinking ever done in the boardrooms of baseball.

In conjunction with the league presidents and the club owners, the commissioner decreed that there should be a "second season," with the winners of the first half playing the winners of the second half. If a team won both halves of the split season, then it would engage the second-place team in its division to decide the division title. This asinine scheme meant there would be intradivisional play-offs before division leaders could be determined. While some club owners and TV networks rubbed their hands with glee at the prospect of a double set of play-offs, baseball purists and people with just plain common sense winced at the perversion.

The bare-faced stupidity of this scheme was borne out when the two teams with the best overall record in each division failed to qualify for the play-offs—Cincinnati in the West and St. Louis in the East. "It stinks," said Reds Manager John McNamara. "An atrocity," said Cardinals skipper Whitey Herzog. Correct on both accounts, but still no cigar. John and Whitey and their players watched the double-tiered play-offs and World Series on television.

The Dodgers, assured of a play-off berth by dint of their half-game edge over the Reds on June 12, coasted to a 27–26 record in the second half and then made ready to take on Houston, winner of the western division's "second season," to produce a contender in the West. The Dodgers won the series, thanks to some fine pitching by Jerry Reuss.

In the East it was Philadelphia versus Montreal, the division's bridesmaids the past two years. This time the Expos got across the altar, putting Canada in the championship series for the first time.

The Dodgers and Expos battled down to a fifth game. With young Valenzuela pitching for the Dodgers and Ray Burris for the Expos, the two teams went into the ninth inning tied at 1–1. With two out in the top of the ninth, Dodger outfielder Rick Monday drove a 3–1 fast ball from Montreal ace Steve Rogers over the center-field fence, making a chilly day even colder in Montreal. The Dodgers held on for a 2–1 victory and their seventeenth pennant, most by a National League club.

And so the game's most bizarre season ended on a note of pure baseball—a championship game, the ninth inning, a tie, a home run, and a pennant is won. It was a home run to go down in league history with the historic blows struck by Gabby Hartnett in 1938 and Bobby Thomson in 1951. And it was typical of the quality of the baseball being offered by the game's "senior circuit" for decade upon decade.

For a while it looked as if there would be no pennant race in the National League's western division in 1982. The Atlanta Braves, under new skipper Joe Torre, broke away from the pack with a record 13 straight victories before losing their first game. After that, it was pretty much a game of catch-up for the rest of the division.

At the end of July, the Braves, powered by the long-ball bats of Dale Murphy and Bob Horner, were nine games ahead of second-place San Diego and ten ahead of third-place Los Angeles. What happened in the next two weeks was utterly astonishing. The Dodgers swept two full series from the Braves over the course of consecutive weekends and suddenly found themselves in first place. The Braves kept losing ball games as steadily and effortlessly as an October elm drops its leaves, running their collapse to 19 losses in 21 games before stumbling back onto the highway to the promised land.

As the schedule dwindled into September's long shadows, the Braves, Dodgers, and Giants found themselves in a three-horse race for the division title. The final weekend of the season saw the Braves scheduled for three in San Diego and the Dodgers and Giants facing off for three up the coast in San Francisco. The Braves had a one-game lead over each of their pursuers. By Sunday, the Dodgers had eliminated the Giants and the Braves had won twice. So it came down to the last day of the season with the Braves needing either a victory or a Dodger loss to cinch the title.

The Braves lost, but so did the Dodgers, on a dramatic three-run homer in the bottom of the seventh inning by Joe Morgan, at thirty-nine years old still a lethal clutch performer.

By the time Atlanta had taken its first division title since 1969, the St. Louis Cardinals had beat off challenges from Montreal and Philadelphia to take their first division title since the inception of divisional play.

Meticulously put together by Manager Whitey Herzog, the Cardinals did it on speed, pitching, and defense. Their 67 home runs was the lowest team figure in the major leagues (Atlanta's Murphy and Horner popped 68 between them). St. Louis had some steady stickers in George Hendrick (19 homers, 104 runs batted in) and Keith Hernandez, Lonnie Smith, and rookie Willie McGee, and the game's most dazzling fielding shortstop in Ozzie Smith. Whitey's boys swiped 200 bags, most in the league. The team's secret weapon was named Bruce Sutter, their sterling relief pitcher. The bearded righty, who featured a split-fingered fast ball that dropped with diabolic abruptness, won 9 and saved 36, giving

him a split-fingered hand in 45 of his team's 92 wins.

Philadelphia's Steve Carlton was the league's only 20-game winner, the thirty-seven-year-old lefty ringing up a 23–11 record, which he garnished with 286 strikeouts. Montreal's Al Oliver, acquired earlier in the year from the Texas Rangers, took the batting crown with a .331 average. It was a satisfying conquest for the quiet, little-publicized Oliver, for more than a decade one of the game's steadiest batsmen.

The championship series turned out to be a cakewalk for the Cardinals, as they rolled up the Braves in three straight, bringing home a pennant to St. Louis for the first time in 14 years.

If the Dodgers' artistic season had been flawed by a single game's deficit at the end, their financial success was no small compensation. The Los Angeles club smashed their own big-league attendance record by drawing over 3,600,000 customers, an average of nearly 44,000 per game. It was a remarkable season-long performance by the West Coast pioneers, ample evidence that 1981's strike had been forgiven and forgotten by the fans. The evidence, in fact, was league-wide, with virtually every club improving its per-game attendance average over 1981.

Once it had been overshadowed by the American League, which had Ty Cobb and Tris Speaker and Walter Johnson, and then Babe Ruth and Lou Gehrig and Lefty Grove, and then Bob Feller and Joe DiMaggio and Ted Williams. But slowly, gradually, thanks to its introduction of black players after the war, the National League began assuming the role of the power league, the glamor league, the place where the stars were. It became the league of Jackie Robinson and Willie Mays and Ernie Banks, of Henry Aaron and Frank Robinson and Roberto Clemente, of Bob Gibson and Sandy Koufax and Juan Marichal, of Pete Rose and Johnny Bench and Tom Seaver and Steve Carlton and Mike Schmidt.

It began in a New York City hotel room in 1876. It began with people traveling by horse and buggy to watch the National League play on irregular diamonds surrounded by little wooden grandstands. And today, in this age of high technology and domed stadiums and carpeted playing surfaces, people are still coming to watch the National League play. Baseball has grown and expanded and gotten better; yet it has never become old. Look on the field and you will see young men with the same goals and aspirations of the young men of a century ago. Watch them. Marvel at them. And know this: As it is today on a baseball diamond, so has it been always.

Al Oliver.

Joe Morgan when he was with the Houston Astros in 1964.

Ralph Garr, National League batting champ with a .353 for Atlanta in 1974.

Tony Perez.

Steve Carlton winding up . . .   . . . and delivering.

Dave Concepcion.

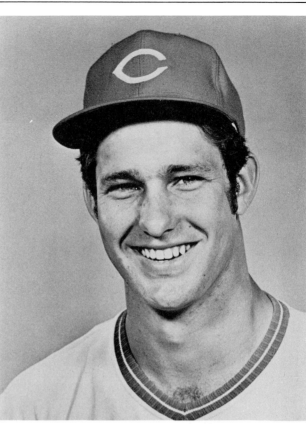

Don Gullett.

Johnny Bench about to be called out at home by umpire Tom Gorman. The catcher is St. Louis' Ted Simmons. The action took place in July 1972.

San Diego's Nate Colbert, who on August 1, 1972, hit five home runs and drove in 13 runs in a doubleheader in Atlanta.

Bob Watson.

Roberto Clemente about to connect for his three thousandth and last big-league hit. It was a double off of the Mets' Jon Matlack on September 30, 1972, at Pittsburgh.

The only three men ever to hit 40 home runs apiece for one team in a single season. Left to right: Atlanta's Darrell Evans, Dave Johnson, and Henry Aaron.

Ted Simmons.

Tug McGraw.

Richie Zisk.

Phil Niekro.

Dave Cash.

Houston's Cesar Cedeno making a game but unsuccessful effort to pick one off of the center-field wall.

Ken Griffey.

George Foster.

Andy Messersmith.

Willie Stargell.

Dave Parker.

John Candelaria.

Bill Buckner.

The Astrodome in Houston. The world's first indoor ball park, opened in 1965.

Steve Garvey.

Dodger catcher Steve Yeager.

Davey Lopes.

Dodger third baseman Ron Cey forcing Pittsburgh's Frank Taveras at third.

Reggie Smith.

Burt Hooton.

Bill Russell.

Don Sutton.

Tommy John.

Dusty Baker.

Tom Seaver.

Larry Bowa.

Mike Schmidt.

Mike Schmidt sliding safely into third.

Greg Luzinski.   Garry Maddox.

A tense Gary Matthews taking his lead off second.

Vida Blue.

Manny Mota. His lifetime 150 pinch hits are the most in baseball history.

Bill Madlock setting his sights on a high pop fly.

J. R. Richard.

Rollie Fingers.

Bert Blyleven.

Gary Carter.

Jack Clark.

George Hendrick.

Dave Kingman.

Steve Rogers.

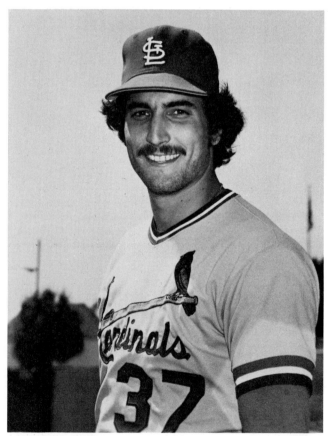

Andre Dawson.

Keith Hernandez.

Dave Winfield.

Pete Rose.

Bruce Sutter.

Nolan Ryan.

Kent Tekulve.

Garry Templeton.

Joe Niekro.

Bob Horner.

Fernando Valenzuela.

Tim Raines.

"As it is today on a baseball diamond, so has it been always." A baseball game in progress at Cooperstown, New York, in 1903.

Index